WHITE MASK

A RE-CELEBRATION
OF MY FIRST NATION HERITAGE

A MEMOIR

WESLEY SHENNAN

Hi Elaine!
June 30, 2020

Enjoy this!
When you look
at my
references,
you are the
third one at the
top of the list!
You'll have to
read to see
where you appear
in the
narrative.

Looking forward
to your book.
Blessings to you &
family. Wes

 **FriesenPress**

Suite 300 – 852 Fort Street
Victoria, BC, Canada V8W 1H8
www.friesenpress.com

Copyright © 2014 by Wesley Shennan
First Edition — 2014

All rights reserved.

ISBN
978-1-4602-4752-5 (Hardcover)
978-1-4602-4753-2 (Paperback)
978-1-4602-4754-9 (eBook)

1. Biography & Autobiography, Personal Memoirs

Distributed to the trade by The Ingram Book Company

TABLE OF CONTENTS

PROLOGUE

THE SUMMER OF 1957 WAS HOT AND DRY, I was ten. When I woke up one late August morning, the sun felt like it was shining right through the cedar shingles, the exposed rough-sawn rafters, and into my feather mattress.

As I lay there, I could hear Sam Cooke singing *You Send Me* downstairs on the tall brown mahogany battery radio, which stood between the log home's two windows looking south toward our dirt driveway. I heard Gramma pulling a drawknife with both hands through a split birch log. She pushed her stomach into the log and held it firmly against the coal and wood stove's chrome edge. After three or four quick crackling draws with the sharp knife, the stove-length log had enough shavings attached to it to easily catch fire in the fire box. When I came downstairs, I saw four brown eggs looking eager to be cracked in the black cast iron frying pan. I knew Gramma would sprinkle salt on the stovetop once the fire got going so our bannock toast wouldn't stick and burn. As she was standing on the leaf-patterned light green linoleum floor in her bare feet wearing a faded blue floral print dress, she said "did the heat wake you up?"

"I guess so."

"My man, today we have some work goals."

"Gramma, what are work goals?"

"They are the things we want to do today."

Seems pretty hot to be working, I thought, while nodding my head, indicating I understood all about work goals, when really I didn't.

She said: "Today, we're gonna fix the fence so the cows don't get on to the road; then we're gonna dig some potatoes for supper; fix the leak in the chicken coop; and, we have to take lunch to Grampa cutting and stooking oats out in the field before he gets too hungry."

After breakfast, Gramma covered her wavy black hair with a red paisley scarf, tied it at the nape of her neck, changed into a pair of faded brown gabardine pants, and put on a long sleeve blue and white checkered shirt. She told me to put my jeans on with a long sleeve shirt so my arms didn't get scratched in the bush and to watch out for the wild rose that could scratch right through my shirt. We headed out looking for the hole in the barbed wire fence strung through a thick grove of poplars. While we were searching, Gramma stopped suddenly, turned to me and held up her palm. She closed her eyes. While angling her chin slightly upward she slowly inhaled. I took in a cautious breath too and smelled an odour similar to our small dog Tippy.

We didn't stand there long. "Did you smell anything back there?" asked Gramma as we continued searching for the gap. I said I smelled something that reminded me of Tippy. She laughed. Gramma didn't think Tippy could smell like game since he was just a house-dog, but she went on to say that we both smelled a deer. We didn't see him, but we could smell him. Gramma said the deer was probably lying down and didn't move. We didn't pose a real threat.

We found the two bottom runs of the three-wire fence on the ground near the road. I guess the cows managed to push it down for the fresh grass in the ditch because the fence was stapled to a few poplars in that section. While I held the wire in place Gramma nailed new staples to the trees, but she said we would have to come back another day and dig a hole for a fence post to fix it properly.

We brought Grampa his fried egg sandwiches a little past noon and came back to dig potatoes in her half-acre vegetable garden.

Wesley Shennan

She said we should get out of the sun and forget about working on the roof of the chicken coop because it's just too hot.

"Weren't we supposed to fix the leak in the chicken coop today, Gramma?"

"Only if we can fit it in. Since it's too hot, we won't do it today."

If we couldn't complete all of our goals in one day, Gramma explained, we can always go back later in the week. She said we shouldn't forget about our goals, but we don't have to worry if we couldn't complete them all today. She said she usually has goals that fill her week and are rarely completed in one day.

"*Humph*," I thought.

I was beginning to understand how goals worked. *So, some goals we have to do, like feeding grampa......he wouldn't be too happy if we put that one off until tomorrow! But I guess others, like fixing the chicken coop, can move around and wait for a better day ....or maybe when we just felt like doing it.*

While Gramma changed back into her cooler floral dress and was crocheting a large white table cloth in the house, I went outside in the shade and practiced throwing a hunting knife at a plywood target I made. When I came back into the house, Gramma was already peeling the potatoes for supper. She put the potato peeler down on the blue and red linoleum counter top when she saw me. When I looked at her I could see the seriousness in her deep brown eyes.

"Sit down, my man. I think you are old enough now for me to tell you this."

I put the long-handled tin drinking dipper back into the pail of cold water on the washstand beside the green screen door and sat down at the dark brown and round oak table. Gramma wiped her hands on her stained white apron and sat down across from me. She sat with her forearms resting on the edge of the table and wove her fingers together between us. Looking at her fingers first, then into my eyes, she asked, "did you know you are part Indian and that we are living on an Indian Reserve?"

I was stunned. My head was spinning. *Wow! I'm an Indian?* I felt an immense surge of pride and happiness in knowing more about who I was; I felt taller, browner, confident. I thought my friends would look at me with a new respect. I couldn't believe it!

Gramma sat there looking at me with a slight grin, but with a concerned look in her eyes. I didn't know it, but she knew my life would never be quite the same again. It wasn't.

Wesley Shennan

1. GROWING UP IN TWO PLACES

I GREW UP IN BOTH ROSSDALE AND THE Michel Indian Reserve. Rossdale was a working class, inner-city neighbourhood in Edmonton where I lived with my parents and went to school. The Michel Indian Reserve, located about 30 miles Northwest of Edmonton in the country, was where I spent many weekends and school vacations with Gramma and Grampa, my Mom's parents (along with my aunt Betty, who was only five years older than me).

Rossdale is widely considered the birthplace of Edmonton. Not only is it the home to the historic Fort Edmonton and Edmonton House, first constructed in the flood plain of the North Saskatchewan River for the fur trade in 1801, but it is also an historic and prehistoric campsite, ceremonial site, and burial ground for First Nations going back 8,000 years, according to archaeological finds and scientific dating. Called Pehonan (meaning meeting place) by the Cree, and part of the Wolf Track, the northern extent of a north / south trail used by the Blackfoot, this sacred ground in Edmonton's river valley predates the ancient Pyramids of Egypt by a long shot – almost 4,000 years.

When I lived there in the 1950s and '60s, it felt like Donald Ross, the first European settler, had just sold his 70 acre farm and green houses. There were large open playing fields everywhere. Renfrew Baseball Park, rebuilt after a fire in 1950, had a new concrete grandstand (with the original wooden bleachers remaining on each side of the new grandstand), and it could seat 6,500 people. Inside the ballpark, there was over 400 feet of well-manicured grass down to the dark green wooden centre field fence. Outside the park were dirt and grass parking lots, a playground with swings, teeter totters and a maypole right beside another square city block of the soccer pitches and softball fields of Donald Ross Elementary School. Two blocks to the northeast was Diamond Park, the hockey rink and speed skating oval, which was another big grassy field in the summer, as well as home to Royal Canadian Shows, a traveling circus that occasionally came to Edmonton. The beavers gnawing on balsam and aspen poplar next to the river were probably doing so for centuries and the songs of chickadees, white throated sparrows, and robins gave 'the Flats' a feeling of being in the country, as opposed to an inner city neighbourhood.

The City of Edmonton Firemen had a training school next to the river at the south end of Rossdale. I remember my friends and I cheering for Mr. Prather, our local Rossdale hero, when he jumped off the pale yellow three-storey tower into a black round flat net held by eight trainees all dressed in their dark blue uniforms. Sometimes the acrid smoke created by the firefighters hurt our eyes and we would cough and run through the thick blue haze to the chain-link fence to watch them training. When they weren't there, we climbed the fence. Once I remember running down the steps of a training building and falling from one floor to another through a missing tread. I was lucky I didn't get hurt, but it happened so fast it almost felt magical. Wolf's Taxidermy, another building just around the bend in the river to the east from the firemen's training centre, was an old two-storey house with all the rooms removed and covered in chalky white paint. At this favourite haunt, it was a real treat seeing moose brains in a pail or receiving an old tooth from Mr. Wolf himself. Wolf's Taxidermy had a strong odour, but not strong enough to make you sick. I enjoyed watching a plaster mould come alive over a few weeks as a White Mountain goat staring at you with coal black eyes. The

North Saskatchewan river flooded many houses in 1952 and again in 1954. I think Mr. Wolf moved his business after that, and I remember the old building being pulled down one day, all that remained was a pile of scrap lumber with clouds of dust rolling over the riverbank. The Arctic Ice plant, an old gambrel roof barn structure with peeling white paint and a faded red sign was nestled amongst the houses on 100 Street and 97th Avenue. It had a stable for horses for delivering ice to homes (even though refrigerators had mostly replaced iceboxes when I was a kid). The stable was a fun place to run around, but I didn't spend a lot of time there. Mom said I might get ringworm if I kept playing in the horse stables, plus there was this weird little German kid, Ralph, who would run around in the stables naked. I still recall this same strange kid approaching John and Ed Monilaws, and I waving a hand-held flagpole which had a large red flag with a big black Swastika on it. He looked like he was trying to scare us because he kept saying "the Nazis are coming, the Nazis are coming." I walked up to him and pushed him over on the boardwalk sidewalk and said, "take that Nazi." Ralph ran home crying with his flag in a scraped arm.

The Rossdale Power Generation and Water Treatment Plants were next to the river right behind Renfrew Ball Park. The original power plant was constructed in 1903. In 1930, a three storey steel, concrete, and red brick rectangular structure was constructed with seven large smoke stacks all in a row for the coal-fired boilers; it looked like a dry docked ocean liner. Philip Lovell, my buddy, always referred to the building as The Titanic. In 2002, a number of buildings on the site were declared a Municipal Historic Resource, as there are only a few remaining examples of early industrial architecture in Alberta. When I was younger, cinders from the seven stacks would cover the snow and get into my eyes, but by 1955, natural gas replaced the coal fired boilers and the air improved considerably. By 1967, the water treatment plant expanded and soon there were industrial-looking cylindrical water settling tanks surrounded by berms and chain-link fences behind, and creeping up beside, the baseball park. There was a rumour about some local kids who would climb the fence and swim in the tanks, but I think it was the stuff of urban legend. None of my friends would be silly enough to swim in tanks with constantly turning blades at the bottom. In summer, we swam in the outdoor pool at Queen Elizabeth Park, just across the Fifth Street Bridge on the south side. In the winter, we went to the pool at Victoria Composite High School on 101st. Street and Kingsway. We only fished in the river, where I usually caught suckers that pulled the hook well down into their throat (I never did catch that elusive Sturgeon). I can't remember anyone swimming in the mostly dirty and fast flowing water of the North Saskatchewan, although I was told about a guy who once swam to the south side, which may have been another urban legend.

Uncle Bill, my dad's brother-in-law, was a grader operator for the City of Edmonton. In the 1950's the streets in Rossdale were made up of gravel, which required constant maintenance. Whenever he graded the streets, I became the envy of my friends running along the street while I sat beside my uncle dressed in his dark green serge shirt and pants, up in the cab of the bright yellow grader, where he taught me about blade angle and leaning front wheels.

On the weekends, Bill (I usually didn't call him uncle) would take me for rides on the gas tank of his silver *Aerial* Square Four motorcycle. I remember oily blue smoke coming from the tail pipes of cars in front of us, looking at the traffic crossing the intersection at 97th avenue and 103rd street and feeling the wind in my eyelashes, as Bill pulled out, shifted and roared passed all the cars. Dad had a motorcycle too, a black *BSA* 350 with a chrome gas tank. I remember riding between mom and dad when at four years old as Bill and Bessie (my dad's sister) rode beside us on our way to Spruce Grove and the farm where dad grew up. I liked looking over at Bessie and Bill as the shiny chrome shocks on the front wheel let the tire move up and down over the bumps while Bill's black leather gauntlet waved at me.

When my friends and I were a bit older, probably 11 or 12, we built forts and formed teams for rock fights down by the river. The rule was to not throw above the shoulders, but of course, someone would run home with a bleeding forehead. I remember making slingshots from a forked willow tree branch, tying pieces of cut inner tube from a car tire to the forks and making a small leather pouch for ammunition. The best ammunition, by far, was a marble. You could kill a sparrow from a good distance with a marble you wouldn't have hope of killing with a rock. Making our own zip guns was fun too, using blockbuster firecrackers. You could buy firecrackers easily back then at the corner store where you bought pop and chocolate bars. There were small red firecrackers called lady fingers, about half an inch long, that you could light and let the whole string go off at one time – they sounded like a series of rapid shots from small calibre pistols. There were medium-sized firecrackers, red and sometimes green about two inches long, which you could set off in a string. Those sounded like the bigger gun-fighter guns in the movies. The medium-sized ones were expensive and it was more fun to carefully unwind the paper fuse strings and blow them off separately, especially if you wanted to plant a few in the side of an ant hill.

I remember Bruce Alexander lost sight in one eye. Someone said he was being a tough guy by holding a medium-sized firecracker in his outstretched hand while it went off. Our favourites though were the orange, red and black striped blockbusters, which were about four inches long and fit nicely into a piece of water pipe. The black iron water pipe was threaded on one end, and after you put the firecracker in the pipe, screwed a nipple on with a small hole for the fuse, and slid a marble down the barrel, you had a ready-made zip gun. The gun propelled a marble about four feet until Richard Rutar said "let's rip up small pieces of paper and ram them down on top of the marble."

"Why?" we all asked him.

His mouth curled down as he turned his palms upward. "Haven't you watched cannon fights in the old pirate movies? They always ram paper or something on top of the cannon ball to hold it tight at the bottom" (I don't think he used the word fodder).

We piled pop bottles three high in a pyramid; rammed small pieces of torn notebook paper on top of the marble with a thin willow twig and lit the fuse. I'm sure they heard us hooting and swearing across the river when one of the pop bottles in the pyramid, 12 feet away, shattered into stucco glass.

At about this same age we liked to visit the Alberta Legislature, constructed in 1911 and resembled a large wedding cake with its domed top and Greek columns. It was located just above the Flats on the top of the river valley to the west. We were usually on our best behaviour there. Once, I was fishing at Calling Lake, located about 100 miles northeast of Edmonton (the only lake I can remember seeing pelicans), with my Uncle Bill and my dad. I found this old rusted bone-handled knife on the shore. I donated it to the museum section of the legislature (back before there was a provincial museum) and was always proud to show my friends a caption that read: "Old Indian knife found at Calling Lake, donated by Wes Shennan."

The three story red brick building where I lived wasn't lined up along the street with a number of other buildings, but instead, looked more like a lonely clone of thirty foot mature balsam poplars standing in an open field. The Ross Flats Apartments, declared a Municipal Historic Resource in 2001, was a thirteen suite apartment building called "The Block" in the '50s. The three levels of grey wooden verandas connected by stairs on both ends of the block were used for meals on warm summer nights by a few new European Canadians (most of us thought it was a little weird: why would anyone want to eat outside when they weren't camping?).

We used the verandas for playing hide and seek (mom said she counted 26 kids living there in 1947 when we moved in) for odd jobs like painting furniture, washing hand laundry, or just sitting in the sun – but never for the intended purpose, thankfully, as a fire escape. The Block had a plank board sidewalk out front along with two birch trees on the boulevard, as well as two tall fragrant lilac shrubs beside the wide concrete stairs. The banisters at the front entrance led up to double dark brown wooden doors with inset glass panels and an ornate brass door handle with a thumb latch. Immediately behind the doors were black, white, and grey terrazzo flooring with the date of construction forever imbedded – 1911. The interior stained and varnished dark brown fir staircase, right in the centre of the building, rises an open three stories, topped by a pyramid-shaped skylight.

One Christmas morning our parents let us fire our cap-guns on all three levels of the stairs, the blue smoke from our toy guns rising to the skylight, but that was an exception. The basement had a laundry room where everyone stored their own wringer washer and you could go out the basement door and up the concrete stairs toward a stand donning six long clotheslines on pulleys strung across the backyard. I always got caught running on the stand and grabbing empty clotheslines to see just how far I could fly in the air.

South of the building was a near acre of flower and vegetable gardens. Most everyone in the block had a garden. Half a city block beyond the clotheslines to the west was the dirt parking lot right up to Renfrew Baseball Park. To the north, a full city block of grassy playing fields of Donald Ross Elementary, where I was schooled. The one and two story houses of the "flats" were mostly across 101st street to the east, but there were three older two-story balloon frame pale yellow houses with green trims east of my home and next to Renfrew's parking lot. The big Vandomselaar family lived in one and an equally big Vandergaag family in another – Dutch immigrants who came after World War II.

"Welcome to the low-rent district," my dad said to my aunt Bessie and I as we stood outside on the second-level veranda of the block. My dad, as usual, was offering his sardonic opinion of "The Block," which I didn't always appreciate. That was the only time I remember aunt Bessie visiting. My dad piled us all into his four-door, two-tone dark green and white 1954 Chevrolet and took us to Banff for a short vacation. Aunt Bessie, in her seventies, had naturally grey curly hair and there was no mistaking her birth place of Kirkcudbright in Scotland, with her thick brogue and odd names for things. "A creek is called a 'wee burn' Wesley," she said rolling the "r," and making the "s" in Wesley sound like a "z" as we crossed a small bridge near Banff.

Back on the veranda, I gave aunt Bessie, an excited nine-year-old's running commentary about the tall Manitoba maples lining the streets of the Flats. I also told her all about Mrs. Cossey's amazing sweet peas and peonies in the back garden beside our own boring corn and potatoes; my two-storey red brick elementary school, built it in 1912 with steep triangular green roof gables and two tall chimneys, where I had just completed grade four; the high dark green fence and wooden bleachers of Renfrew Ball Park where, next Summer, I hoped to sell programs and cushions. I told her about the angled Hotel MacDonald (also built in 1912), with an eleven story centre section, perched on the top of the North Saskatchewan River Valley and overseeing Rossdale like a Scottish castle, like a picture I saw in a book of Edinburgh castle in Scotland.

In the spring, I remember my dad on more than one occasion coming home during lunch hour to guide the milk man's horses that had trouble pulling the heavy open-topped yellow milk wagon through the muddy ruts in the alley. The milkman, dressed in an air force blue uniform and policeman-style skip hat, sold red tokens, which he carried in a brown leather bag held by a wide shoulder strap. If you weren't home at delivery time, you simply left your clean glass milk bottle in the hall with the red token, which fit nicely into the top of the bottle. If you didn't have tokens, you could just leave coins in the bottle.

But, of course, it wasn't always that simple. I remember catching a little German kid, Klaus, dressed in a burgundy ribbed wool sweater with buttons on the top of one shoulder, steal our coins. "Owwww," he yelped after I pushed him against the wall, punched him in the stomach, and caught the milk bottle with the coins still inside just before it hit the floor.

"Don't ever come back you little bugger."

He yelled something as he ran crying out the front door of "The Block,", but I knew he wouldn't be back. For the most part, he was an exception.

There was also a bread man who delivered 22 cent loaves of bread about every second day. I remember Mom saying "every time we get a good milkman or bread man they always get a promotion, and then we are stuck with these guys who can't even make change." At 22 cents, they probably ran out of pennies and tried to round up. The bread man sometimes received his payment in an envelope left outside the door, but bread delivery didn't seem to last as long as milk delivery. You can still get milk delivery in Edmonton in the 21st century (not by horse-drawn cart mind you).

Rossdale and "The Block" were much lonelier places in the winter. There was often four feet of snow and ice on the streets for up to six months of the year. We moved three times into the old building. When I finally got my own bedroom, the plaster walls were wet with condensation when at minus 40 degrees, which happened every winter for at least two or three weeks. I just went to school and stayed inside when it was that cold. I couldn't even go skating. My feet would get too cold and the ice felt sticky.

"Here you go, Wesley," said Uncle Bill through his steamy breath as he got out of his brand new green and white Rambler Rebel with "pullmanized" seats, handing me his old shin pads in the winter of '57. They were made of enormous, thick white felt, a series of thin bamboo stocks sewn in black leather sleeves to protect your shins, and a cumbersome piece of thick tan-coloured leather sewn over the knee cap. They were so large they felt like goalie pads. I really wanted to play hockey and use them, but I got cut during the community league try-outs. "You can't skate well enough," said coach Randy Solohub as he watched us at Diamond Park. I lent my pads to my buddy Peter Schurman, who used them a lot after he grew. I kept skating without pads and a stick.

In my early teens, I spent many Friday and Saturday nights at the community rink playing "crack the whip." A long line of guys and girls (I always made sure I was holding onto a girl) would hang on to each other's waist and skate around the rink until we were going pretty fast, then the guy in the lead, usually Pete Schurman, would turn around, quickly join hands with the person behind him, and at the same time, put on the brakes and pull for all he was worth. This transferred energy all the way down the whip to the last guy who was immediately sent flying at a very high speed. If you were a good skater you could usually stand up, but a poor skater often fell, and depending on the length of the whip, could be hurt a little as he went hurtling into the boards.

Another time I was skating at the speed skating oval at Diamond Park, and to this day, I have one front tooth pushed farther into my mouth than the other. I was hit by a speed skater in full flight. I remember him saying to his partner, "I could have killed him," as he gave me his handkerchief to sooth my bleeding face. Meanwhile, I couldn't believe I was stupid enough to make one of my fancy turns right in front of him as he rounded the corner at 25 miles per hour.

If you didn't skate, play hockey, curl, or ski you spent most of the winter indoors in Edmonton. After being inside for so long with short days and long cold nights (the sun would go down about 4:00), winter became a depressing time. But I knew it wasn't just the winter – there was always something about the old block that made me feel uneasy. Like I was being watched.

――――

Michel Callihoo signed Treaty 6 on September 23, 1878 on behalf of his "Cree" band of Métis relatives. He was the son of Marie Patenaude, a daughter of a Northwest Company employee (Michel Patenaude, and his Cree wife Francoise). His dad was Louis "Karilo" Kwarakwante/Callihoo, a well-known Iroquois

Wesley Shennan

Freeman who made his way 4,000 kilometres west, all the way from Kahnawake, Quebec with the fur trade in the early 1800s. Michel's brother, Jean Baptiste, was my great, great grandfather, which makes Michel my great, great uncle. But when I trace Gramma's lineage, Chief Michel is also my great, great grandfather! Intermarriage made Gramma and Grampa cousins because their grandfathers, Jean Baptiste and Michel Callihoo, were brothers.

As described in the *Indian Act*, a band of Indians were to make their homes on designated lands called "reserves," (or the Rez to use a modern colloquialism).When originally surveyed in 1880, Michel Reserve 132 was forty-nine square miles. Survey maps from 1903 and 1904 show a rectangle of eight miles by six, bordered by the Sturgeon River to the north, and located approximately nine miles due west of the St. Albert Settlement. The Rez contained Atim Creek (Dog Creek in Cree) flowing through the southern half and a number of small lakes scattered throughout. A large portion of the north had the best number two black loam farmland in Alberta. In the 1950s, when I spent most of my time there, the Rez was smaller and the hamlets of Villeneuve and Calahoo were located along the railroad crossing the Rez on a diagonal from northwest to southeast.

I didn't know it was an Indian Reserve until I was 10, and like my mom, I continued referring to it as "the farm." Michel Reserve was indeed a farming community. Grampa, or Solomon Timothy Callihoo, who was born in 1898, and Gramma, Lottie (Charlotte Emma) Callihoo (nee Fyfe), born in 1902, built all of the buildings on the farmstead with Uncle Dan Laderoute, the brother of Grampa's mom. Gramma said she wanted Tamarack logs set in sand for the base before building the rest of their two-storey home of local balsam poplar logs. After it was built, Gramma would chink the logs every year with a mixture of clay from the Sturgeon River, a little sand, some water, and a small amount of calcimine to make it stick. She always made sure the chinking was brown, like the logs, and never added too much of the white calcimine. The steeply pitched roof, constructed of rough dimension lumber rafters and cedar shingles, made sleeping on the second floor easy. My dad once said he slept the clock around, 12 hours, lying on a home-made feather mattress and pillow, covered in another home-made feather duvet, and allowing the lightly falling rain soothe his slumber.

House Of Solomon and Lottie Callihoo, Michel
Indian Reserve, Alberta, Circa 1950

Norbert "Preacher" Callihoo, Solomon Callihoo,
Lottie Callihoo, Betty Callihoo, & Elizabeth
Callihoo (nee Collins), circa 1950

Wesley Shennan

The farmstead also had a six-stall log barn for cows with a flat roof sprouting grass, a small chicken coop made of balsam poplar logs, three or four granaries made of dimension lumber with cedar siding, an outdoor water well, and a pit toilet. There was also a single car garage framed over a narrow trench in the ground, which allowed Grampa to work under cars and trucks.

Uncle Johnny, who at the time I didn't know was Chief John Callihoo, a prominent First Nation leader in Alberta with a plaque in his honour on the wall of the Alberta Legislature, wanted Grampa to look at his poorly running big black Desoto sedan. After asking Uncle Johnny about the engine burning oil and a compression test, Grampa said it needed a valve job.

"You can do that?" said Uncle Johnny.

"Uh-huh," said Grampa, typically using as few words as possible. After a week the job was done. Uncle Johnny had a daughter, Lydia, and a grandson, Barry, who was my age. Quite often they would take the short cut through our yard and stop to chat and drink tea. One day, while Barry and I threw hunting knives at trees, Uncle Johnny was back in the house likely discussing enfranchisement, as he seemed more serious than usual. Years later, I learned the Michel Band was the only Nation in Canada to enfranchise under the *Indian Act*. This part of the Act has been abolished, but the old Act allowed Indians to sign a piece of paper, which instantly made them non-Indians. Enfranchisement allowed them to drink in the bars, (after you showed your letter or light blue "Certificate of Enfranchisement" card), and to vote in federal elections (Indians weren't allowed to drink in bars or vote in Canada until 1960). The last Michel Band enfranchisement was in 1958, and families were enticed by a cash settlement of around $20,000 each to sign. It was another way to "de-Indianise" Canada.

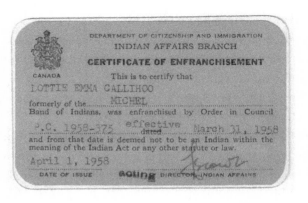

Gramma's Certificate of Enfranchisement

A few years after signing, there wasn't much change around Gramma and Grampa's place, except that they now owned the land, a quarter section, as the whole Reserve was wiped off the map and replaced by privately owned deeded land, registered in the Alberta land titles office in Edmonton. Gramma and Grampa also acquired a few shares in mineral rights under some land next to Gladu Lake. The Michel Reserve had really become just "the farm."

Grampa continued to clear his quarter by knocking down the trees and hauling them off to the fence line. There were still lots of roots to pick, and I spent many days pulling roots and stacking them in piles to burn to help him. Grampa also rented quarter sections from neighbours to expand his grain farming enterprise.

It was about this same time that electricity came to the area.

"How come that pole at our driveway leans into the road, Gramma, and the rest of them are all lined up straight along the road?" I remember asking.

If power was connected to the house, Gramma explained, the tension on the wire would pull the pole straight and line up with the others along the road.

I asked Gramma when we were getting electricity.

"Oh they came around," she said, "but I told them we don't need any electricity around here."

At night, I liked the hiss of the mantle lamp while we listened to the battery operated radio. I would help Grampa by cutting the four tailor-made cigarettes from one long one in his factory roller. I remember really enjoying a slice of Grampa's bread (baked bannock) and jam before going to bed. When it was bed time, Gramma would light a wick oil lamp and lead us upstairs. One evening we came home late during a spectacular thunderstorm and immediately knew something was different—there was an unfamiliar sulphur-like odour when we opened the door. Gramma had a picture of Jesus on the wall upstairs and we saw where the lightening came through the peak of the roof, burned a line down the wall and around the picture of Jesus, went down my metal bed post, and burnt a small hole in the linoleum floor downstairs, where it made the big coal and wood stove jump closer to the outside wall. Another time, I think, we were out late picking saskatoons and choke cherries (I never liked picking berries and being eaten by all those mosquitoes) and the house had been swarmed by bees. Grampa calmly filled his sprayer with DDT and went about the house spraying. We went to bed after the hum died down and got up in the morning to continue killing bees with fly swatters.

Grampa's brother Uncle Vic, Auntie Bea, and their large family lived on the adjacent two quarter sections to the east. Their farmstead was modern compared to Gramma and Grampa's. They had a two-storey frame house with a white siding and a green trim, as well as a number of out buildings, including a large red gambrel-roofed barn with a hay loft. My mom said Aunt Bea organized a dance in that hay loft for her marriage to my dad, but it rained so hard that all the dirt roads on "the farm" became impassable in the spring of 1946.

One day, Aunt Bea and Uncle Vic's oldest boy, Clifford, borrowed Grampa's dark green Oliver tractor (which had no fenders over the large back tires). Vernon, one of Clifford's younger brothers, jumped on the tractor and they drove down the road together. I think Clifford lost control of the tractor when Vernon showed him a comic book and the tractor flipped over in the ditch. Clifford died. He was pinned under the large rear wheel, but Vernon lived, having fallen on the spinning upper wheel and thrown against a power pole. Shortly after, I think it was only the next year, both Vernon and his youngest brother Curtis died in a fire that destroyed the two-storey family home. It's interesting what you remember about people – to this day I can still hear Curtis laughing—short small coughs that made me laugh too. All I remember about Vernon was a red bent wood willow plant stand he made, which Aunt Bea kept in the basement of her new home.

Years later, Wayne, who is my age, told me he and his brothers woke up during the fire, formed a human chain by joining hands, and made their way to an upstairs window. Wayne said his brothers weren't holding his hand when he got to the window. He reluctantly jumped to escape the thick smoke, which poured out of all the windows and doors.

Although Wayne is my Mom's first cousin, he is more like my first cousin. I liked visiting and spending time with him and his remaining family (his Mom, Dad, and little sister Joyce) who built a new house across the road from the original farmstead. His oldest sister Eleanor had already moved from home by this time. I think it wasn't too long after the new house was built that Uncle Vic died. I remembered him as a kind, happy man who liked to dance. A few years later, I learned he was an alcoholic who fought death, but had to give in. He died of cirrhosis of the liver in his '50's. Loosing half of his young family to accident and fire probably didn't help his addiction.

Wayne and I shot at least a thousand gophers with our .22s, and drowning them with pails of water drawn from the well. When they came up their second hole, we stabbed them with a hunting knife. Wayne had Shetland Ponies and we used to ride them, but I didn't ride much as they were mean and, when you weren't looking, would sneak up and bite your triceps. One day we were asked to each carry a pail of water and a pail of oats across the road for the horses. That day, I learned water was almost twice as heavy as oats, even though they were being held in pails of identical size. Wayne laughed while he let me carry the two pails of water.

Aunt Bea had a great sense of humour. One time, Wayne and I were riding in the box of her 1952 blue International half ton truck on our way berry picking with Gramma and Joyce, when she hit a pothole in the road. The water was deep and splashed through the hole in the floorboards holding the gas pedal, soaking her new white sandals. After her initial surprise, she had to stop the truck because she was laughing so hard.

Visiting neighbours was a tradition on the Rez. Aunt Lena (Emmaline, nee Callihoo) and Uncle Willie Dubis, would come a long way by horse and buggy from Namao, usually on Sunday after church. Aunt Elizabeth and Uncle Dick (Solomon) Callihoo would visit by horse and buggy, too. I remember they would both tie their horse to a small clone of trembling aspen in the front yard so that the animal had some shade and could graze on the grass. Sometimes we would visit Uncle Fred and Aunt Mary and their adopted son, Joe, by car. One day, on our way to visit them, we stopped at Sammy Callihoo's place; (at least I think that was the name Gramma said). What I do remember was dodging chickens as we pulled into the front yard and noticing a lot of litter. There were very few out buildings and the home was a log structure chinked with clay, something like Gramma and Grampa's, except it was only one storey. There were blankets hanging as room dividers inside where too many children lived in that small house. That day I decided to wear my beige jeans, a light brown checkered shirt, and black leather, western-style jet boots. The boys were probably wearing the only clothes they owned – faded T-shirts, GWG (Great Western Garment Company) Red Strap blue jean bib overalls, and scuffed low-top leather boots with laces. Gramma and Grampa seemed to be discussing something serious and we didn't stay long (thinking back, it could have been enfranchisement). I was happy to leave early, feeling very uncomfortable in my slick city clothes with eight dirty dark-skinned kids saying nothing and staring at me.

We continued on our way to Uncle Fred and Aunt Mary's, who lived in an unusually narrow two-storey frame home across the railway tracks a few quarter sections to the south of gramma and grampa's place. They had their prized television set under the stairs. I remember there was no television when I was younger. The first television broadcast from Edmonton wasn't until 1954. We knew television was coming though, and my dad used to tease me and tell me that if I looked into the light on the combination radio/ record player at home, I would see an announcer with a big nose.

After leaving Uncle Fred's that day, I asked Gramma a few questions.

"How did Joe get such a good sun tan?"

"Well, some people are born with a good tan,"Gramma answered.

"Oh," I said, "Is Uncle Fred a Chinaman?"

"No, he's your Grampa's brother."

"But is he a Chinaman?"

"No, he's your Grampa's brother."

Both answers were unsatisfactory, but I didn't know how to probe or express myself better. Gramma knew too, and a few years later when I was 10, she revealed information that affected me for the rest of my life, in more ways than I could ever have imagined.

We liked to socialize and party. Informal gatherings at Gramma and Grampa's would often result in us moving the big round oak dining table back into the corner so we could dance. The music was live, with Gramma and Grampa playing the fiddle and me or my mom accompanying them on guitar. My aunt Betty could really dance the red river jig, but she was married at 15 and left home so young that I mainly remember her dancing after she was married. When there was a break from dancing, we would sing country songs in three part harmony along with the guitars. I remember social drinking mainly, and only a few drank too much, Uncle Vic being one of them before he died.

Sometimes the gatherings were more organized. I remember once travelling with Gramma one-half mile to the next quarter section west where the large Calahoo family (they spelled their name like the town) had moved into a former schoolhouse. I can't remember the number exactly, but I think Roderick and Alice had fifteen children. Gramma thought it was funny when I repositioned her beret so it was on an angle instead of pulled straight down over her brow. She said she was covering her hair so it didn't get dirty during the clean-up before the big dance. I said she looked nicer with it on an angle. She couldn't wait to mention my fashion sense to Alice, because it didn't make any difference to her how she looked.

During that dance, I met Brian St. Germain who played guitar better than me. I sat and watched while he accompanied the different fiddle players. When it was gramma's turn to play, she wanted me to accompany her. I always liked seeing people dancing to our music, I still do.

There were L'Hirondelles, St. Germains, Callihoos, Calahoos, Loyers, Fyfes and La Bontes, as far as I could remember, and we were all related in some way. I was even related to some of the guys there not born on "the farm," like Uncle Robert, my dad's youngest brother. This was a big dance. I remember having to walk home a half mile in the dark after midnight with Gramma because Grampa was busy pulling drunk drivers out of the snowy ditch with his new two-tone green and white 1956 International half-ton truck. We could hear the tires squealing in the dark while Gramma said "the old man is going to drive our nice new truck into the ground." I thought she was right, as the squealing was endless, and I could imagine the blue smoke from the tires blocking out the light from the headlights of the car in the ditch.

A farmstead I really liked was Lloyd Callihoo's, about a mile and a half northwest of Gramma and Grampa's near the Sturgeon River. Lloyd's house, if I remember correctly, was a square two and one-half-storey balloon frame home with dormers. He also had a big gambrel-roofed barn like Aunt Bea's, but it wasn't painted red. His out buildings, like the home, were all allowed to weather to a natural silver-brown colour. I think Lloyd was focusing on being a grain farmer instead of a mixed farmer. His equipment—the tractor, harrows, plough and seeder—were all lined up and ready for use. Everything seemed neat and in its place. The only animals around were a few horses in the barn.

I met a fellow on the Rez named Sonny, who Dennis and James (two of Roderick and Alice Calahoo's 15 children) said could really play the guitar. We rode our bicycles over to Lloyd's one day and all five of us proceeded to play guitar in Lloyd's living room. Sonny really could play. I had never met anyone before who could play fiddle tunes on the guitar. He could softly double pick the 32nd and 64th notes like he had a bow in his hand. One of his favourites was **The Old Man and the Old Woman.** I could keep up chording, but that was it. I did enjoy playing with him though, as he was subtle and never aggressive in his delivery.

Another time, Sonny, Dennis, James, Wayne and myself rode our bicycles south across the tracks beyond Villeneuve, to Buck and Nora Jones's place (their name was Callihoo too, but they seemed to like the name Jones better). They had a son my age, Gary, I believe, who wasn't healthy. I think he had rheumatic fever when he was small and it damaged his heart so he couldn't run around with the same energy as the rest of us. His mean dog sneaked up behind us while we were leaning on our bicycles and talking, and it bit right through Sonny's jeans through to his cowboy boot so that he broke the skin on his calf. Sonny swore while Gary laughed. That summer, I also remember attending a wedding reception in the basement of Buck and Nora's new home for their daughter Cookie (I never knew her given name). She married a guy by the name of McFadden from Manville Alberta and all I remember about the reception was Gary's practical jokes and the extremely rough finish of the new basement. It looked like the forms were constructed of crooked pieces of plywood with leaking edges leaving rough seams at odd angles all over the basement walls.

I guess Sonny and Lloyd practiced their guitar playing, as I saw them perform at the talent show held at the Noyse Hall in Calahoo a few weeks later. Dennis and James wanted to attend the talent show and I asked Gramma if I could go with them. Gramma told them both to "just watch him." We hitched a ride with Dennis and James's older brother Donald.

Dennis and James had other plans. As soon as we arrived at the talent show they wanted to go somewhere else. I jumped out of the car because I spied what I thought was Aunt Bea's 1952 blue International, but to my surprise Aunt Bea was nowhere to be found. Just as I was beginning to panic, I felt a friendly tap on the shoulder with the words: "Hey young fella, what are you doin' here alone?" To my relief it was my Uncle Robert. He was there with his buddies, Haas and Gordon Callihoo, and planned to stay the whole night for a big dance after the talent show where Francis Callihoo, one of the best fiddlers around, was playing with his band. "I can give you a ride home after the dance," Uncle Robert assured.

I think one of the talent show winners was a blond guy of about 20 who sang the Johnny Cash song *I Still Miss Someone*. I really liked it, along with Johnny Horton's *Spring Time in Alaska*. A few years later, the Johnny Cash song became a regular part of my repertoire. Sonny didn't win anything and was really disappointed. I tried to cheer him up and said he should play a little solo with Francis later at the dance, but I could have mentioned I thought

Lloyd's chording was way too loud. I guess Lloyd was nervous and kept flashing his friendly under bite smile to the crowd while strumming stronger and harder. Poor Sonny, meanwhile, was furiously picking away, but no one heard a note from his subtle acoustic guitar.

My Uncle Robert, Haas, and Gordon danced, drank, and in Gordon's case, kissed the night away. Gordon and his cute blond girlfriend stayed in Haas' Mercury while the rest of us went to the dance. When there was a break in the dancing, my uncle would tease Gordon and say "Well, will you look at that, kissing right in front of God and everyone!" At the same time, Haas opened the hood of the Mercury and extracted a mickey of rye whiskey hidden beside the radiator. I thought it was a really cool idea to hide your liquor under the hood, so when the cops stopped you and asked "have you got any liquor in here?" you could honestly answer no. As Haas showed me, even if the cops lifted the hood, it was so well concealed you'd never see it.

About two in the morning, Haas's Mercury rolled into Gramma and Grampa's yard. I thanked Robert (I usually didn't call him uncle) and scurried into the house. Gramma seemed a little worried, but she didn't scold me. I think she was more relieved than anything as I wasn't more than 11 years old. She was more upset with Dennis and James for letting me get out of the car. But as Dennis said: "we watched him for as long as he was with us."

Gramma and Grampa kept farming until 1965 when Grampa turned 67. They sold the quarter (160 acres) for $15,000, if I remember correctly. A few years later, the new owner became very wealthy as gravel was discovered throughout the whole area around Villeneuve. The new owner even contacted Grampa and Gramma, who were now living in a small home in Milk River south of Lethbridge. He said he planned to farm and was surprised as anyone about the rich gravel deposits and gave Grampa and Gramma another $3,000.

Other than hunting ducks, grouse, and rabbits, skinning the rabbits and feeding them to the pigs, and swimming in the Sturgeon river with Grampa (who looked like a sparrow, a big upper body supported by skinny legs), my memory of the Michel Reserve is just as I've described. My life experience as an individual, however, is continually unfolding and surprising me now, in how closely it is tied to these roots.

2. MUSIC: STARTING FROM THE WOMB

WHEN I WAS FOURTEEN THERE WERE TWO paths: sports or music. Although I liked skating and baseball (downhill skiing became a passion at eighteen), singing, playing guitar, and playing drums and percussion, remained number one in my heart, and came dangerously close to being my whole life.

My first exposure to music was from in the womb. Mom said she would play her brown acoustic arched top *Playtime* guitar with "f" holes and sing country tunes like *Have I Told You Lately That I Love You* "without a care in the world." After I was born, she said I would fall asleep in the afternoons to the classical music broadcast from CKUA radio, playing on the combination radio/record player in our little bachelor suite.

The very first melody I can remember was a popular tune when I was four. Mom and dad took me to the old Misericordia hospital on 110th street and 98th avenue, for a three-day stay, because our whole family was ill with tonsillitis. The remedy in 1950 was to remove both your tonsils and adenoids. The anaesthetic was memorable. The nurse in her wrinkled green scrubs said "I'm just going to spray this up your nose," but a brown rubber aspirator bulb flew from her hands and across the room. Although I didn't feel great, I still let out a surprised chirp and wondered if flying rubber bulbs were part of her plan. She ran across the room, picked up the aspirator bulb, and said "okay, this time it's gonna work." She quickly sprayed something up my nose and I was instantly surrounded by a black galaxy filled with twinkling stars, slowly floating down and down and down in my safe little white crib. When I awoke in recovery an hour later, the nurses received me with their reassurance and asked if I wanted anything. I had a sip of water, but after they took me to my room immediately asked "could I please have some ice cream?" I think they liked a kid with manners, but I had to spit out the first spoonful. They laughed and said "everyone wants it, but it always tastes really bad because of the operation." My dad told me the next day the ice cream tasted really bad because of all the blood in my throat. He was right about that. I remember coughing and spitting large clots for the first couple of days. I also recall asking for a tomato sandwich and eating it, and dad couldn't believe the tomato didn't burn my throat. I sat up straighter in my bed and felt tough.

I don't think they had radios in the room, but there was a speaker system in the hall, mainly for announcements, and in the evening they would play music. That was when I first heard Anton Kara's *The Third Man Theme*. Dad told me it was played on a zither and not a funny sounding guitar like I thought. A number of years later, I learned it was a successful score in the 1949 movie, *The Third Man*, and in 1950 had become a popular single played on the radio. *The Third Man Theme* still reminds me of young, pretty nurses in white shoes, white uniforms, and white caps pinned in their hair, joking and feeding me ice cream at the old Misericordia.

I was six when Mrs. Featherstone, my grade one teacher, was listening to us playing in the school yard. She grabbed my hand after recess and took me to every class in the school to sing *How Much is that Doggy in the Window*. She would knock on the classroom door, ask the teacher if we could come in, then she'd point: "stand here" (which was right at the front of the class with the black board behind me). And after: "Okay Wesley, sing for the class." I don't remember being shy, singing a couple of verses of the song and hamming it up with high squeaky barks, "arf, arf," after the first few lines, and I especially liked singing: "I must take a trip to California," because California was probably the biggest word I knew.

After school, Donald Cossey from the grade five class said I sang out of tune, but I just ignored his comment because I knew him (he lived in "The Block) and thought *what does he know, he can't even sing*. At Christmas time, Mrs. Featherstone appointed me as Master of Ceremonies at the Christmas Concert, which was held in the large open square in the middle of the first floor of Donald Ross School. Mr. Edwards, the principal, along with the school janitor, made a stage and strung a black curtain across the front. As soon as the curtain was pulled, it was my job to walk on and introduce the acts. Mom said I was even encouraging the bashful kids by rolling my left hand toward me and saying "come on, don't be shy." The only time I remember being embarrassed was when mom cut a little piece out of the newspaper reading "the concert's Master of Ceremonies was Wesley Shennan, grade one." I made a little cowboy hat from that newspaper clipping so no one could read it.

The first guitar I learned to play was a flat-top brown acoustic Hawaiian, played with two metal finger picks, a plastic thumb pick, and sliding steel. I was eight years old when I started taking lessons at Olsen's School of Music, located in a green and white 1930's gable end bungalow on the top of 103 street near 99ᵗʰ Avenue beside the Ex-Service Men's Home for Children. I enjoyed it, but Mrs. Meyer's lessons were really slow. They were in "high bass," which, if I remember correctly, was an open "G" tuning. When I got a new teacher, Miss Antoniuk, (who in retrospect was "hot," in her tight red dresses and long dark curly hair), I moved upstairs to the kitchen and joined the "E7s" because we tuned our guitars in an open "E" (maybe it was open "E7" I don't remember all the details). I learned why the lessons with Mrs. Meyers moved slowly. I was playing everything by ear and couldn't read a damn note. I just pretended to read notes. As soon as I heard the simple melodies being taught, I was able to play them instantly without learning to read anything – I was something like a parrot, listening, playing and pretending. It was a big surprise when Miss Antoniuk handed me a complex piece of music and asked me to play with the others in our class (there were five of us). I heard four guitars playing harmonies higher and lower than me, and their notes came at different times in the measure. These guitarists simply counted, read their notes and rests, and played at the appropriate time. I, meantime, tried to memorize and hear my tune among their harmonies, play at the right interval, and make everything fit in timing and tone. It was tough. The sheet music helped, but more as a general guide than a real source of what to play and when.

I really wasn't understanding the details of reading sheet music properly. But if we practiced enough, I could hear my part without really reading it. I liked dressing up in a white shirt and black dress pants, playing in our recitals at the Masonic Temple on 103rd street just north of 100th avenue, when Frank Gay, a local classical guitarist and master luthier, would judge our performances. Reading notes, however, was not my strong point. It's still like that today. I'm an 'ear' learner.

My interests in drums and percussion stem straight from "the farm" when Grampa played the **Red River Jig** and other tunes. It's interesting to hear what ethnomusicologist Lynn Whidden says about this music during an interview in 2006, to paraphrase... she says string instruments were in North America for millennia and brought again by Europeans during the fur trade. Percussion sums up Metis playing. They choke up on the bow, use their feet like a drum and violin like a voice. It is an aural tradition, not taught with notes, but by intent, watching and active listening. Ann Lederman a musician writing in 1987 about the Métis fiddle style in Manitoba says: ...to paraphrase, Metis fiddling is similar to French Canadian, but there are monotone endings, descending pitch and once and a while, five-beat phrases which are typical of Ojibwa songs. From this, it is likely the Scots and French fiddle traditions supplanted an existing string instrument culture in North America. The percussive style and phrasing of Métis fiddle music has a distinct First Nation influence.

Learning this type of music is not done by reading notes but by intent, watching, and active listening, which is exactly how I learned it. I remember being five or six years old, rolling around on the floor next to the worn black wooden rocking chair runners, and watching Grampa's brown leather shoe on his right foot rock back and forth, heal to toe, heal to toe, and hit the floor in a solid eight beats per measure. He only used the toe of his left shoe, which would strike the floor on four beats per measure. He planned it, however, so that the left toe struck the floor immediately after the right toe. The rhythm I heard under the fiddle tune was like a galloping horse. I practiced and was soon able to copy Grampa's galloping rhythm. I could beat it out by adding my heel instead of my toe, which Grampa sometimes did too, and carry the same rhythm by drumming my hands on the round oak table. I liked doing it along with the music. You could hear me in the corner drumming on the table, and at the same time, hear Grampa's feet hitting the linoleum on the plank floor – like surround "stereo" beats to the fiddle music.

A few years later, when I was eight or nine, I learned to play the Spanish guitar from mom (at the same time, I was learning the Hawaiian). The Spanish guitar was a little more difficult to finger than simply sliding a steel up and down the frets was, but I liked it better (and I didn't have to read notes, bringing back to the aural tradition). Soon I was able to accompany Gramma and Grampa for waltzes, jigs, reels, and schottisches. As Ann Lederman mentions in The Canadian Encyclopedia, ...to paraphrase, until 1960 fiddling was the principal source of dance music in rural Canada. It is one of the country's strongest and most original musical traditions dating back to the 17th century. Oddly enough, I never even thought about playing the fiddle. I guess it never really appealed to me. Today, when I listen to contemporary fiddle music from Quebec, played by groups like La Bouttine Souriante, it has the same galloping rhythm. But what surprised me were the Latin/Afro-Cuban rhythms, many of which seem to have exactly the same beat; the clave clicking in time with Grampa's left toe.

In 1956, when I turned ten, Elvis Presley came on the radio with his monster hit *Heartbreak Hotel.* I remember dad and mom asking Bessie and Bill "what kind of music do you think this is?" They talked about it for quite a while, which isn't surprising, as it really was something new, with the drum and stand-up bass emphasizing the two and four back beats, and the twangy guitar solos. Today we have categories like Rock 'n Roll and Rockabilly, which was mostly what Elvis was playing in the early years, but when he first broke onto the music scene with this big hit, he was really quite unique, combining country with its Celtic roots, as well as southern African-American rhythm and blues. Mainstream radio, especially in Canada, had not played anything quite like it before, except perhaps Elvis' earlier songs, but they weren't as big a hit or as popular as *Heartbreak Hotel.* Finally, in frustration, my aunt Bessie declared "Oh, he's just country," but mom and dad weren't so convinced. They could hear something different, but couldn't quite define or decide what it was.

Around the same time, I was introduced to more African-American music when Ted (I usually didn't call him uncle) gave me his collection of Meade Lux Lewis records. I can still remember they were larger than normal 78s, neatly packaged in a thin card board box cover, with stylized black pianos drawn over a yellow background. I listened to that boogie-woogie piano over and over. I hadn't heard anything like it. I am pretty sure it was Ted who instilled that never ending crescendo of jazz music in my life. Ted grew up in the city and married my dad's sister Helen, who grew up on a farm north of Spruce Grove near the Michel Reserve. On the Rez, I played our music, but in the city I was learning about jazz, just before the rock 'n roll revolution took hold of us all.

Initially, I played in a rock 'n roll band we formed at McKay (pronounced McHigh), my Junior High School. We called ourselves the Serenaders, although we didn't serenade anyone as we were a guitar band playing popular tunes we heard on the radio like *Dance On* by the Cliff Richard and the Shadows. My best buddy Brian MacKenzie, Morris Wittiuk, and I took turns on lead guitar, with Skip Couture on drums. Brian, Morris, and I went on to play in other bands, but Skip didn't. I don't know if it was a conscious decision or not, but he seemed to enjoy being an outrageous delinquent more than music. He once "borrowed" a pack of razor blades from a downtown drug store and proceeded to cut the nipple off his right breast. I guess he was showing us how tough he was (because he was quite short); or maybe it was a secret cry for help by mutilating himself in public? Whatever it was, it was memorable.

Another time he was upset because he failed a grade, so he went outside and shot the top floor windows out of McKay with his .22 rifle. The cops had little trouble figuring out who it was, as they projected a line from the holes in windows back to where the bullets entered the ceiling and then looked down the straight lines that lead to Skip's back porch. When I was in High School, I heard Skip was already in a federal penitentiary in Kingston. I didn't know if it was true, but I wouldn't have been surprised.

Morris Wittiuk's Fingers, Brian MacKenzie, Skip Couture
& Wes Shennan, McKay Avenue School, 1961

After playing with the Serenaders, I joined a rock 'n roll band known as The Barons, sometimes called The Casuals. We must have been known more as The Barons since our glossy white business cards had the name front and centre written in blue stylized print, and at the bottom: "call Ken Avison." Ken was our leader, a magician as well as a drummer/musician. He worked at the magic shop on 98th street and just down Jasper Avenue from the Hotel MacDonald near the Dreamland Theatre. During band practice sometimes, he would entertain us with his most recently acquired illusion. Will McCalder, on sax and piano, eventually became "Willie" of Willie and the Walkers, a popular '60s and '70s band in Edmonton. I played lead guitar and wrote a few tunes that sounded a lot like the Venture and Fireball instrumentals we were mostly covering, like *Vaquero, Torquay,* or *Gunshot.* Not too surprising, since I was taking "ear" guitar lessons from Bob Clarke, the lead guitar for Edmonton's best cover band in the '60s—The Nomads.

Bob was recording (in Clovis, New Mexico under the direction of Norman Petty), when he was with Wes Dakus and the Rebels, an Edmonton group that wrote a number of original tunes as well as playing covers. There he met George Tomsco of the Fireballs, a band from New Mexico. George and Bob enjoyed playing together as they explored the nuances of surfer-style guitar. This was around the same time Bob wrote and recorded one of his most popular instrumentals *Las Vegas Scene*, which had some airplay on Edmonton Radio stations like CJCA and CHED.

Bob liked to teach all the new stuff he was learning and had a wicked sense of humour. One day I was at a lesson in the Award Guitar School, a small single storey grey stucco commercial building on 95th Street just off Jasper Avenue, when Bob said "let's go down the hall and listen to Hank Smith pick like Chet Atkins." Bob was blond, about five foot seven, and was wearing white jeans and a navy and white paisley shirt. I got a faint whiff of his *Brute* after shave as we went into the studio at the end of the hall to listen to Hank playing his big red country *Gretsch*, holding his breath while getting through the tough parts, then gasping when they were over. Bob said "we had to come to see if you were alright, we thought you were drowning." Hank didn't think it was as funny as we had.

There were a host of Barons who came and went, including Morris Wittiuk, or Mouse as we sometimes called him, who apprenticed to be a Ford mechanic right out of high school. Lowell Seymour, a guitar player whose dad played drums in a Dixie land band, who also owned a Jaguar with leather seats and a back window that looked like a mail box slot, (we played the role, driving up to the front steps of the community hall like rock star celebrities); Brian MacKenzie, my best buddy who was unflappable, didn't like to sing much, but played rhythm guitar as consistent as a drum beat; Dave Peters, who grew his hair, dyed it white, and became Lil' Davey of Davey and the Drasticks, another '60s cover band in Edmonton. Later, we had a girl singer, Marilyn, who seemed to like Ken a lot.

The guy in the band who influenced me the most, however, was Tony White. He brought vocals to the group and we evolved from playing The Ventures covers like *Walk, Don't Run*, to playing rhythm and blues such as Chuck Berry's *Roll Over Beethoven*. The vocals made us come alive. We got a series of gigs at the Pleasant View community hall for their regular Friday night teen dances. We played for a graduation dance at Garneau Junior High, had a gig out of town in Winterburn (where Tony put his heel through an amp doing a kick dance), and we even played for free at a Sunday afternoon charity fashion show. Things were happening! It was exciting to make people dance to our music and get paid too. Tony could sense our success and started to make plans.

Community hall teen dances were where the average bands played. The better groups like The Nomads, Wes Dakus and the Rebels, The Lords, and The Saratogas (the group where Barry Allen honed his singing before he joined Wes Dakus and later The Privilege) played at the Rainbow Ballroom on Whyte Avenue, Club Stardust at the Highlands Community Hall. Or else they played at local lakes, like the Lake View pavilion at Cooking Lake, Mameo Beach Hall at Pigeon Lake, or at the Alberta Beach Hall (before it burnt down) on Lac Ste. Anne. The early '60's were more conservative and formal, with the guys in the bands wearing form fitting suits and skinny ties, much like the early Beatles. The dancers were just as formal, with the guys usually wearing slim fitting suits, white shirts and skinny ties, and the girls in dresses, perhaps a bit more revealing than they would wear at school, but not by much, and high heels. I was playing with the Barons and attending dances at Club Stardust with my buddy Brian MacKenzie in 1962 and can't recall any serious fights or disagreements. Everyone seemed to be enjoying the music and just dancing.

By the mid to late '60s the whole scene changed. The guys in the bands grew their hair, had beards, and hardly ever wore anything resembling a formal suit. You didn't see ties on anyone. The dancers were the same and had evolved to wearing jeans, sneakers, and short sleeve sweat shirts or open neck shirts with a few buttons undone and cowboy boots for the guys; or, jeans, tight sweaters, and flat leather shoes, or sweat shirts and sneakers for the girls. The farther the dance hall was from the city, the wilder the time.

Lake View pavilion at Cooking Lake was a favourite haunt of ours in 1965 and '66, and to keep order they hired bouncers. I had never seen or stood beside men so big and strong. The tallest guy I ever stood beside was Warren Champion, a basketball player at high school, about six-five and probably weighing a lithe 190 lbs. The bouncers at Lake View were six-seven or taller, weighed at least 300 lbs, and were muscular, not fat. The only thing missing from these guys was the horned Viking helmets.

One night while Wes Dakus and the Rebels were playing a blistering version of the Rolling Stones big hit *(I Can't Get No) Satisfaction*, Brian MacKenzie, Peter Uram, Gordon Harper, Terry Harris, Grant Cameron, Gerry Shea and I had just met our favourite group of girls—Linda Hadley, Inge Stauning, Joan Ullman, and Heather Cochrane—and a big fight broke out in the middle of the dance floor. As the Rebels played on, there were so many kicks and punches you couldn't make out who was being pummelled (thankfully no one seemed to carry knives or guns), but it looked like Pete was down on the floor getting hammered. I was standing beside Terry. He said, "I've got to get in there and help Pete."

"Those bouncers will kill you," I said.

"I know, but Pete's getting hammered!" he answered.

I remember thinking *but Pete's not a fighter*.

Soon as Terry waded in and grabbed the guy on the floor (and discovered it wasn't Pete underneath getting punched, but a Métis guy wearing the same orangey-brown sheep skin jacket with a wool collar), a bouncer grabbed him by the scruff of the neck, stood him up, turned him around, and squeezed his cheeks together hard with one hand. While continuing to squeeze Terry's mouth with his one hand, he calmly walked and pushed Terry backwards out through the main doors. Terry stumbled free outside and was told to "bugger off." Terry, who was six feet tall and weighed about 180 pounds at the time, was no match for this guy, but being the resourceful fellow he was, simply took off his tweed sweater, put it in the car, messed up his hair, and walked back into the hall a few minutes later wearing his plaid shirt. When he came back in he said "I was saving that asshole?" while pointing to the Métis guy. I remember thinking *the guy's not a lesser human being, but I'm sure glad I don't look as Indian as he does*, a teaching "infecting" my whole family that I did not learn about until years later.

At Lake View another time, while the Nomads were in the midst of a searing cover of the Beatles *Long Tall Sally* with lots of people dancing (after drinking too much bootlegged rye, beer, wine, or anything else they could get their hands on), I remember a guy about six-one, weighing around 200 pounds, and standing near the fence (separating a few rows of tables on raised flooring at back of the hall). He had rolled up the short sleeves on his tight black T-shirt and stood, arms akimbo. You could tell he lifted weights regularly, and his flexed biceps and demeanour told everyone he was looking for a fight. One of the super-sized bouncers walked up and hit him with a lightening quick left jab to the mouth. The bouncer backed up, smiled, stretched out his hands palms up, with his fingers saying, "okay tough guy, let's go." The tough guy's chest heaved with anger as the blood seeped from the corner of his mouth, but he didn't dare move. He found what he was looking for, but the outcome was all wrong. I enjoyed watching this reverse bullying spectacle unfold through the smoky haze, the thumping twelve-bar bass and the non-stop sweaty dancers in time with the back beat.

Lake View pavilion was run-down by the '60s, but I really liked the interior design. All the flooring was maple hardwood and there were a series of dark green French doors that separated the large dance hall from the coat check, concession, and sitting area with over-stuffed dark brown couches and a fire place. I could almost feel the '40s and hear Glenn Miller playing *In the Mood* while guys in military dress uniforms and girls in frilly dresses did the jitterbug.

But back to Tony White. One evening he invited us to his place and said "don't bring any instruments." His parents didn't approve of his rock 'n roll. Occasionally my parents agreed to store his instruments at our place – a heavy dark-brown *Gibson* tube amplifier and an off-white *Fender Telecaster*, with one too many character scratches. Tony was the type of guy you wouldn't expect to see in a rock band. At six-two, strong with blond curly hair, and probably 250 pounds, he looked more like an out-of-shape football player than an avid rock 'n roller. Most guys in rock bands had my physique – five-ten with tight black suits clinging to every joint of our 130 pounds.

Tony was very serious on this particular night as he invited us into the basement rumpus room, complete with linoleum glued to the concrete floor, fake palm trees, and velvet paintings of sunsets. He said playing music was a business and if we got really good at it we could make loads of cash. We could have recording contracts, and after a couple of years, the records and royalties would keep the money rolling in. He was serious. It may have been his body language, the setting, or the way he talked about earning loads of cash, but we couldn't stop joking around. After one too many puns, he berated us and said "Oh, come on you guys, can't you see this is serious business?" After we settled down he posed the big question: "Okay, who's ready to hit the road and become professional?"

Will McCalder was holding Tony's dog and said, with an equally serious expression in his voice, "Well, I don't know Tony, it's about this dog." We all split our sides laughing and couldn't stop. Poor Tony was beside himself. We left shortly after. His words, however, reverberated like his old *Gibson* amp.

I don't know if Will even finished high school before touring extensively with his own band Willie and the Walkers, and they secured a recording contract with Capitol during this time. A few years later, he became a founding member of the Powder Blues, a group that won Canada's most prestigious music award in 1981, a Juno. Today he is well-known headline blues man, playing in

Vancouver mostly. Ken joined another guy from the flats, Wolf Krider, and they formed a band that toured and sounded quite professional compared to The Barons. I think they called themselves the Emeralds for a while. Tony, meanwhile, was really serious about becoming a professional showman. He formed a group that also toured and played cover tunes. One night I heard them in a large gymnasium on the south side and, although they had a tight sound, I felt embarrassed for these guys. While fat Tony gyrated to the beat on rhythm guitar, the poor skinny lead on Tony's shoulders was swaying back and forth trying desperately to play a complicated riff high on the neck. I can't even recall the name of the group (maybe it was the Kingsmen?). It was the only time I heard them and probably the last time I ever saw Tony.

Tony's speech reverberated within me still. I thought seriously about practicing more and learning to sound more professional. I really enjoyed the challenge of learning more complicated pieces, even trying to write a few of my own.

It is interesting to look back at the choices we've made, and how they affect us for the rest of our lives. When I was twenty, I worked in a ski resort for a whole season instead of becoming a commercial airline pilot. That decision came down to which job I was offered first, working at the resort or driving a delivery truck in Edmonton while learning to become a pilot with the Edmonton Flying School at the municipal airport. Sometimes I wonder what I could have been, if old Fred McDowell at Lake Louise didn't call and ask me to drive into the Rocky Mountains and become a ski lift operator in November 1966.

A few years before Fred's call, I had made another big decision at age fourteen to not become a full-time professional musician with Tony White. It was a path I came very close to following. I sometimes muse about another life that never was, but when I watch movies like *Backbeat,* a story about the early Beatles in Hamburg, I can identify with parts of it. But the movie actually reinforces my decision not to become a full-time musician. It was

Wesley Shennan

the lifestyle, not the music, that helped me decide. I didn't even know about the serious drug culture waiting around the corner. I was primarily thinking of playing one-night stands in smoky bars and dance halls from Edmonton, through Saskatchewan, Manitoba, and on to Toronto, while living in a run-down van, travelling all day and playing all night, waiting to be discovered by some guy with a big cigar.

The exploitation of young musicians, touched upon in *Backbeat*, was something I wanted no part of. When I compared that lifestyle to most of the guys in The Nomads, who held regular day-jobs and played locally on the weekends, I decided the road show wasn't for me. I wanted to stay in school and keep my career options open. I could still play music full-time if I wanted to, but I refused to be a dropout musician. In retrospect, I know I made the right decision for me. Being in the vortex of "sex, drugs and rock 'n roll" probably would have been more than I could've handled and would've finished me long before now. Years later I would learn why I didn't have the confidence to handle it.

3. SUMMER OF '63

THE HIGH MÉTIS CHEEK BONES, LONGISH
black wavy hair, olive skin, and full breasts made her look older than
her 14 years, but no matter how I looked at her, one word kept pushing
itself to the surface – jail-bait. Her name was Darlene Reiling. When
she attended our teen club meetings, she never took her eyes off me.
With a slim mischievous smile, she would turn her head slightly to
the right, and proceed to probe my soul with both eyes.

I was sixteen, Vice President of the Rossdale Teen Club in 1963,
and Leo Kuta was President. The Club met in the community hall
on the corner of 97th Avenue and 102nd street, a simple gable-end
structure built in the late '50s, plastered with grey stucco embed-
ded with broken green bottle glass. The windows had heavy home-
made iron mesh on the outside to discourage vandals, mostly local
young kids who smeared the word "fuck" in stolen paint on the
parging just below the stucco. The hall's main feature was a shiny
maple hardwood dancehall floor the same width as the interior, 40
feet, and extending back 70 feet to the kitchen and bathrooms.
We sat on grey metal fold-up chairs. Leo and I, with Donna, the
Secretary-Treasurer, had our backs to the kitchen breeze-through,
while sitting at two ¾ inch plywood fold-up tables placed between
us and our 50 club members. In the spring, Leo, his girlfriend, and
I attended a few workshops organized by the City of Edmonton,
teaching us about efficient and solvent clubs, and with our newly
acquired knowledge, we came back and organized teen dances to

raise funds. If we raised enough money, maybe we could help build a decent rink shack with a bathroom. Our meetings had minutes and motions like, "all in favour of holding a dance on the first Friday of next month," and "all in favour of Donna being in charge of contacting the band for the next dance," which felt important, but those soul-searching eyes always distracted me with their intrigue.

The Club broke even and sometimes made close to a hundred bucks at a few dances. The community league executive said we had to have adult chaperones so things didn't get out of hand. I volunteered my dad for one of the dances and, to my surprise, he actually seemed to enjoy it. He told me later that he liked the way Leo made sure there were no fights or drinking at the dances, a kind of self-appointed bouncer. I met Leo a few years later at a dance at Mameo Beach. It was no surprise he'd just joined the City of Edmonton Police Force. He was one of those guys who kept growing after high school and added another four inches to his six foot frame. Never one to back down in a fight, and at 220 pounds, he made an impressive policeman.

That summer I went to summer school and worked as many hours as I could, keeping score for two baseball leagues at Renfrew Park. One night I was sitting on top of the 12 foot fence at centre field next to the scoreboard when I heard a voice calling my name. I looked down and it was Darlene. *God, she's cute. Why isn't she a little older?*, I thought. She walked around the outside of the baseball park and stood in the tall grass.

"Hey," I teased, "why don't you come up here?"

She wasn't strong enough like my buddies to shimmy up the steel I-beams holding up the wooded fence, but she tried. Another night she convinced the ball boy, Daryl St. Laurent, to trade places with me so I'd be working on the ground. I told Daryl to take a hike. I wasn't going to give up the best job in the park just for her. After the games, she was always there in a short dress and lipstick, not saying much, but moving melodically to a tune she seemed to have in her head. I felt like taking her hand and spinning her around like we were dancing the jive, but I just looked at her curvy legs and feet shuffling in the dust while avoiding eye contact. After a while, when there weren't any baseball games, she started to call me on the telephone. *God*, I thought, *she's cute, but a bit much*. I didn't know her from elementary school or junior high because, like Leo, she attended the Catholic Schools.

Daryl finally said "why don't you stop ignoring her and spend some time with her? She really seems to like you."

"She's too young."

"Ah, what's a few years," he said.

It was late August. The sun was setting earlier, but it was still warm, and the dry weather had cut the mosquitoes out of our lives. It was just at dusk when I decided to walk down to Wing's Grocery, buy a *Hires* root beer and hang out for a while. At first glance, Wing was a typical corner store guy, but after you got to know him, living alone upstairs and opening a rare coin business in half of the store, you knew he wasn't a typical family man speaking Cantonese all night. He liked to talk, spoke pretty good English. He would selectively boot-leg for the older guys in the Flats who weren't quite legal drinking age (which was 21 in the Alberta of 1963). When he moved to Vancouver he sold everything and that's when we learned he owned a couple of walk-up apartment buildings not too far from the store and built just a few years earlier

Darlene lived in a little green and white cottage-roof bungalow down from "The Block" on a 101St Street near Wing's. She must have seen me walking by. When I got to Wing's she was right behind me.

"What are you up to?" she said, right through that little smile. There was more to the question, of course. I felt a slight tinge of excitement as her eyes seemed to reach through and touch my retinas.

"Nothing much, just hanging out," I said, not ignoring her for a change. I wondered if I sounded too excited to see her little curvy body.

She bought a grape *Crush*. "Why don't you walk me back to my place?" she asked.

We didn't say much as we walked along, but I couldn't stop snatching glances at her hair as it bounced, and at the way she put the bottle to her lips to sip her grape pop. *Is she really only four-teen?* I thought to myself. *She looks fantastic. Look how she puts her tongue in the end of the bottle so she doesn't drink too much. God, I find even that exciting.*

When we got to her door, she asked "do you want to come in for a while?"

I knew she lived with her mother and an older sister, who was around my age.

"Sure," I answered.

I knew (or maybe I was hoping?) no one was home. As it turned out, it was just the two of us. We sat down on the long red and beige floral couch, with its back to the picture window beside the front door.

"How old is your sister?" I asked, groping for something to say.

"Oh, let's not talk about her," she said as she slid up beside me.

I really wanted to kiss her, but didn't know exactly how to begin. I moved my left arm from between us and swung it around behind her. She instinctively leaned into me. We cuddled for a while. At exactly the same time, we gently placed our pop bottles on the coffee table, looked at each other and kissed. Her mouth tasted like grapes, but there was more. She tasted exciting as I put my tongue just behind her front teeth.

After a few more kisses we were slowly laying down, her between me and the back of the couch. I started to think, *Okay, little girl, how far do you want to go? Am I calling your bluff, or are you in the lead here?*

Her lips pulled on my bottom lip while I felt her firm, full but-tocks under her skirt. She arched her back toward me. I took it as a message to move my hand from her buttocks to the front. I pulled down the front of her panties and slid my hand past more pubic hair than I had and found a warm moist cavern squeezing my fingers. While breathing in my ear, she reached down with her left hand and began to massage my penis through my jeans. *Holy shit, what do I do now?* I fumbled with the button that held up my jeans, pulled down my zipper, yanked down my shorts, and heard her extended "oh!" as my very erect penis nudged her clitoris.

Just as I was breathing in her scent, listening to her voice, and moving down, a car door slammed. We both immediately sat up. While I tucked myself away as best I could and pulled up my zipper, she pulled her panties up under her skirt. Her mother and her boyfriend walked in just seconds after we sat up.

"Oh, hello, how are you guys?" they greeted.

Without waiting for an answer, they both headed for the kitchen.

"I gotta get some air," I said.

I went outside and leaned on the porch railing. Darlene came out about a minute later. She was smiling, swaying her hips from side to side, holding something in the air and said "look what I found." It was my wallet. When I went to grab it she pulled it away, laughed, and then gave it to me. I looked into the house and no one was in the front room. I pulled her close to me, sucked on her lips and told her "I better go."

It was one of those warm late-August nights in which you wouldn't be able to see anything without street lights. Darlene filled my senses, my thoughts. I felt like running down the street, *I can't go home feeling like this*, I thought.

I went to my buddy Denny Burrell's house to talk to someone and clear my head when Porter, the little black family dog, greeted me. He seemed to like the scent on my fingers almost as much as I did. Jack, Denny's younger brother, said Denny was out with his girlfriend, Leslie Lamont. It was Denny and Leslie who introduced me to Liana, a Finnish airline stewardess. About two years later, over an intense weekend, I completed what I started with Darlene.

Darlene didn't stop phoning me for a couple of weeks. I was fantasizing about having her climb through my bedroom window from the back veranda. I knew it was possible because I did a trial run. It was easy. If she came around the back during the day, it wouldn't be as obvious as walking through the front door of the apartment block. There would be less of a chance of anyone seeing her and we could make love all day, every day, before school started. The thing that weighed upon me most was I knew she would do it! Was I ready to screw a fourteen-year-old every day and take a chance on her getting pregnant? What if she got mad at me and went to the cops? They'd throw me in jail right away, even if she was the one who wanted all this loving. To be honest, she frightened me. She was only fourteen, but her needs and actions were way ahead of her.

After ignoring her again, she eventually stopped calling. Later, I heard she was screwing around with Skip, my outrageous delinquent buddy and drummer with the Serenaders. Was it really me she wanted or just someone to love her? She didn't have a dad. Maybe she just needed male attention?

In retrospect, I've met a few women who didn't have their father's love and really needed a lot of attention, so much so in one case it was almost like an insatiable alcoholic! I've also learned not to feel uncomfortable around teenage girls who like to sit on their dad's laps. I guess it is normal if it is just a father's affection and his expression of love for his daughter (I've never had a daughter, so found this behaviour a little strange earlier in my life).

As for Darlene, I guess I'll never know if it was me she wanted or just love in her life. She moved away about a year later, (someone said it was out of town) and I haven't heard from her since the summer of '63.

Wesley Shennan

4. GORBYS, GLACIERS, AND AN AVALANCHE

"HEY, SHENNAN!" (WE LIKED TO CALL each other by our last names), "I know about this really neat job in the mountains. You live there in little cabins and give guided tours on a glacier." These were the excited words of my best buddy Brian MacKenzie. It was the spring of 1965. I was eighteen years old and working 35 hours a week for Don Fleming at Central Car Park, parking cars in and around an outdoor lot just south of Jasper Avenue on 102nd street, while finishing grade 12 at Victoria Composite High School. Brian was talking to me on the telephone all energized after talking to his step dad Jack Deakin. Jack wrote a column, "Rural Route," for the *Edmonton Journal* and drove to Jasper, Alberta one day after learning there was a glacier right beside the highway about 60 miles south of Jasper town site where an entrepreneur, Bill Ruddy, was involved in a business named Snowmobile Tours Limited. Bill hired young guys to drive twelve-passenger *Bombardier* snowmobiles and give guided glacial tours on the Athabasca tongue of the Columbia Icefields, where a mass of tourists came to Jasper National Park every summer. Brian's mom, Dorothy, was thrilled to learn there were so many young guys the same age as Brian driving snowmobiles and thought it would be a lot better summer job for him than pumping gas at Parliament ESSO on 109th street in the shadow of the Alberta Legislature Building.

Brian wrote the exam and passed the Class A driving test, which allowed him to drive trucks, buses, taxies, and ambulances, and he started work that summer, spieling about the glacier to the tourists, called "Gorbys." I applied that first year too, but I didn't get my Class A drivers' licence before applying. On the application I said I was working on it, but my dad told me "if you really want that job, don't work on it, go out and get it."

It was good advice. The first year Brian was giving tours and I got a full-time job laying sod for a guy in Edmonton, who bounced my pay cheques. It was a good thing the Board of Industrial Relations had a thick file on this guy, because my complaint wasn't the first. I received my June and July pay at the beginning of August. With a few extra bucks in my pocket, I set off for the Columbia Icefields in my two-door hardtop, fire engine red, 1955 Chevy with Sid Sugarman, a friend from high school. Although I had been on many long car trips with my parents, who used to take me camping throughout the north western United States almost every summer, this was probably the first trip on my own. Earlier that year, my dad cashed-in the education insurance policy he bought for me when I was an infant and bought the '55 Chevy. After paying $600 for the car and more than $100 for insurance, there was less than $300 of the original $1,000 policy. I was ecstatic. Although it was a six cylinder with a two-speed automatic power glide transmission, the fire engine red two-door hardtop still looked great. Still, I learned very soon I needed a job to support my car and that's why I was working 35 hours a week for Don Fleming while going to school. The car also brought a whole new social life of dancing, girls, and late nights, all of which coincided with my considerably lower marks in grade 12. Dad never really said, but I think the car was my reward for going so far in school. He wanted to give me something to start my life as an adult (dad only had a grade eight education and mom was home-schooled on the Rez up to the equivalent of grade seven).

Brian wasn't that surprised to see Sid and I when we arrived. There was no telephone service, but Brian and I wrote letters. I told him I was probably going to quit and come and visit him at the "ice". He really seemed to take to his job living at 5,600 feet above sea level in a little compound of trailers and cabins, hiking on the glacier and on mountain trails on his days off, flirting with all the cute chicks who worked at the Chalet (located on the highway opposite the glacier), and making pretty good tips from the Gorbys (as much as his salary on some days, which was around $1.50 per hour with room and board included).

It was an outdoor life that really appealed to me. I spent many hours outdoors on the Rez and on my Aunt Betty's farm in southern Alberta, driving a tractor, hunting and swimming in the river. Only this was better as the mountains were so exciting compared to the flat prairie. There was much to learn about glaciers and climbing in the summer and downhill skiing in the winter, a sport I was keen to conquer.

The winter before Brian got his job at the Icefields, we were introduced to downhill skiing in Edmonton by our buddy Grant Cameron. We were a core group of six guys: Brian and I from McKay Avenue Junior High; Grant and Gerry Shea from the Hardisty/Gold Bar Neighbourhood; and Terry Harris and Gordon Harper from the area around Victoria Composite High School. We hung around with other guys on occasion like Peter Uram and Sid Sugarman, two of the small minority of Jewish guys who attended Victoria Composite.; and Fred Shaw, a Junior "A" hockey player from Jasper Place, who befriended Peter after he moved. Grant and Gerry attended Victoria Composite because a high school wasn't available in their neighbourhood. Before they got their drivers' licences, they were bussed from south east Edmonton, across the Dawson bridge and up the hill to school every day.

Young guys enjoy hanging out in groups and we were no exception. We all joined the Edmonton Ski Club, located on the river bank in Cloverdale, the next valley neighbourhood east of Rossdale. After learning the basics, we were off to the Rockies to really ski. We travelled a lot to Marmot Basin in Jasper National Park. I was thankful to be back working for Don Fleming to finance all these trips. Grant, our skiing mentor, witty and intelligent, is the kind of guy who would show up at your door on Christmas Eve with a gift of ski socks. During Brian's first year at the "'ice," they were short of drivers, so Grant quickly obtained his Class A license and was off to the Columbia Icefields for the last few weeks of the season.

Gerry Shea is a totally different character from Grant. Gerry was more of an observer and thinker than a leader. Although he didn't look like it at six feet tall and 135 pounds at the time, he is actually quite athletic. I enjoyed his self-depreciating humour. He said that when people see him on the ski slopes they probably wonder how three skis manage to make it down the hill, two on the snow and one standing up. He seemed to have more restrictions from his parents and didn't spend as much time with the group as the rest of us. Sometimes Brian would tease and call him tag along Shea. Gerry obtained his Class A license about the same time as I did, so he and I started giving glacial tours during Brian and Grant's second year at the Columbia Icefields.

Brian MacKenzie and I have similar personalities. He is quiet, but not shy. His humour is subtle and often includes puns. He is athletic and caught on to skiing quite easily. He ended up living in Jasper permanently for a few years after working three or four seasons at the Icefields. Once, out hunting, he confessed he couldn't shoot a deer. The "men" in a bar at Jasper proceeded to razz him and he promised himself not to share too many heartfelt feelings, especially with those not close to him. Our friendship today, which spans 50 plus years, is such that it immediately picks up where we left off, even if we haven't talked much for a few seasons.

Terry Harris, a Renaissance man, conquers most things he attempts and had no trouble learning to ski with the rest of us. Although Terry and I were not that close, I know he is generous. He helped me weld the left front A-frame back onto my '55 Chevy when it broke off one winter. He did the brakes on my '59 Chevy – all for nothing. All I did was pay for parts. I don't think Terry had any interest working at the Columbia Icefields, but he is the only one in the group who eventually made Jasper his permanent home.

Gordon Harper I have not talked or heard much from each other since our time together in the mid to late'60s. I remember him as an intellectual, always reading and discussing esoteric subjects. He really enjoyed skiing too, but took too many chances. He lost a number of teeth when the shovel of his ski hit him during a high speed rolling and tumbling fall while attempting to schuss the intermediate run at Marmot Basin. I know he tried to obtain his Class A license a couple of times, but he didn't pass the driving test due to constant speeding. Had he passed the test, I guess he may have driven snowmobile at the Columbia Icefields too, but it wasn't meant to be.

My first year at the Icefields, I drove an orange snowmobile number 12. The twelve-passenger **Bombardier** snowmobiles, made in Valcourt, Quebec and invented by Joseph-Armand Bombardier, pre-dated the smaller machines normally associated with the word "snowmobile" or Ski-Doo today. They were introduced in 1942 (with the last one produced in 1979) and designed for mass transit in the private sector, such as transporting people and food to remote mining and lumber camps and in the public sector as school buses, ambulances, and police cars in the snow. The ones bought for the icefields had rubber tires on the front instead of skies for steering, as we took them on the harsh moraine gravel and over the hard slick ice. They were driven by rubber and steel tracks (riding over four rubber tires per side connected by separate axels), which extended for about three-quarters of the length of the vehicle from the back up to the front doors – something like a military half-track. In the rear was a 318 cubic inch Chrysler engine. You could hear the throaty rumble of the V8 coming out of the exhaust pipes between the tracks on both sides as we double clutched and used the column shifter to slow down. The Gorbys sat on upholstered benches with their backs to the wall, which had four port-hole style windows per side and made the all steel snowmobile look something like a large motorized lady bug.

Brian MacKenzie & Gerry Shea, Columbia Icefields, 1966

Bob Sunderman taught me to drive a snowmobile when I arrived the first year. He was about 25 years old a little shorter than me, probably 5'9" and weighed a fit 180 lbs. I remember thinking how powerful and broad shouldered he looked compared to most of us, who were 18 and 19 and hadn't "filled out" yet. He was a skier, originally from Camrose, Alberta on the prairies, but had worked in the Rockies for a number of years and even drove snowmobiles in the winter with the skies on the front, transporting skiers at Sunshine Village, a ski resort in Banff about 120 miles south of the Columbia Icefields.

Bob took me on the moraine road, which felt pretty close to a 50% (45 degree) grade down to the glacier.

"Hold on to the gear shift in first gear going down the hill. I saw one slip out of gear and we almost had a disaster, because these things are really tough to stop as the brakes aren't that good – they're basically a clamp around the drive shaft to the tracks," he said.

Wesley Shennan

After we got on to the ice he said "don't drive like you're driving your car with your thumbs wrapped around the steering wheel, unless you want broken thumbs. There are hidden pressure ridges on the ice, some that come up overnight, and you can't see them after the ice cutter makes a road.

At first I felt like a primate holding onto the steering wheel that way, but after hitting a few pressure ridges and feeling the steering wheel actually burn in my palms, I soon got used to it. He went on to give me a number of cautious pointers about driving on the ice, but after talking to a few of the experienced drivers, I jazzed-up my driving a little (like parking the snowmobile on a pressure ridge with the front wheels off the ice), to make a few more tips.

There were a number of other guys who had recently graduated from Edmonton's Victoria Composite High School: Bob Melnyk, driving light grey number 16 and Ed Shelenko, driving the fast yellow number 2. We would compete for tips by telling stories and entertaining the Gorbys. After talking to Geoff Murray, a guy who had been there for three seasons already, he said he read *Hot Rod* Magazine and knew the names of drag racers from all over the States. If there was a Gorby from California, he would mention one or two well-known drag racers from California, and the tips would start to roll in. If the first group of Gorbys gave you tips while the second group was watching and waiting to board the snowmobile, you had it made. The chain reaction went all day. I didn't know drag racers as well as Geoff, so I tried to read newspaper articles about the States, as most of the Gorbys were Americans. I remember once telling a group from Chicago about the number of dead fish on the shores of Lake Michigan, which had the scientists in Chicago baffled. I felt like I was from Chicago by the way they kept looking at me and asking me questions. Needless to say, the tips that day were outstanding! I made $12, which doubled my salary. We worked three eight hour shifts – early morning, late morning and afternoon, and a split shift. Quite often we had days off in the middle of the week, which really didn't make much of a difference, as the tours operated during the daylight hours seven days a week all summer. If you needed extra time off, or had to be somewhere for the weekend, you simply traded days off.

Learning about glaciers and their different formations, like moulins or mill holes (where melt water scours a swirling hole in the ice), or a crevasse (not a *crevice*, we would tell the Gorbys, which is a split in rock formation), when moving ice is pulled apart—all of it became an important part of our spiel.

Brian and I went to the public library in Edmonton in the off-season to learn more about glaciers so we could improve our standard spiel. When we were back driving, we learned to balance the twelve-passenger snowmobile over a large mill hole to get a better look at the water swirling down a wide black hole in the ice (as the V8 Chrysler engine in the back made the front end light). If you balanced it just right, the snowmobile would dip farther into the abyss just as the Gorbys came one-by-one to the front to look down.

Of course, the inevitable happened one day when an inexperienced driver, Bill Elliuk, took himself and his passengers right into a mill hole. The terrified Gorbys scrambled out of the large retractable sun roof as the water swirled past the snowmobile's port holes into the gaping black void. Bill lost his job. Gordon Forster and Harold Gordon pulled the snowmobile out of the mill hole with the M5, a vehicle that also had tracks but was larger than a snowmobile. When they started the engine, however, it caught fire. Luckily, they had a fire extinguisher on hand or they would have been down the road too along with Bill.

Another time, I was parked at a mill hole about six feet in diameter with water swirling in from two sides. I had balanced the snowmobile just right so it would dip as the Gorbys came forward and I leaned way out with the driver's door open while hanging onto the light door chain with my right hand (the chain kept the door from swinging all the way open). Suddenly, the metal screw holding the chain to the door let go! My left hand, by my side, moved with cat-like quickness to catch the steering wheel just as I was starting to fall into the mill hole. The surge of adrenalin in my system made my heart pound at probably 150 beats per minute. I could feel the beads of sweat instantly forming on my brow. I just stayed crouched beside the door holding onto the steering wheel for a while, gathering my nerves, taking deep breaths, and thanking God there wasn't a Gorby standing beside me when it happened, as my left hand would have hit the Gorby instead of grasping the steering wheel. From then on, I didn't trust the door chains, but I still balanced the snowmobile over the mill holes. Most of the Gorbys really liked it.

Of course, being around tourists every day wasn't all sunshine. Some drivers convinced themselves they hated Gorbys, but I didn't become that cynical. Other drivers, like Doug Morrow, would make up stories about French explorers and tell the Gorbys in a thick French-Canadian accent about the discovery of the Icefields. One time, I remember spieling at the top of the moraine road overlooking the glacier and there wasn't a cloud in the sky, when the Gorbys kept interrupting and not laughing at my standard witticisms. I thought it may have been my delivery as we were drinking scotch the night before, but usually I got a laugh before we drove down to the glacier. When I balanced the machine over the mill hole, they complained and threatened to sue. While spieling at a crevasse, a guy smoking an ugly green cigar threw it right into the pretty blue formation. I was disgusted and he knew it. When we arrived at the turn around point to let them out for a walk, I tried to scurry off to have a smoke with Gerry Shea, but they demanded I take their picture. I thought: *okay you bastards you asked for it.* This was back in the days of film and you waited days, sometimes weeks, before looking at your vacation shots. I am sure they really enjoyed the shots I took. One only had heads at the bottom of the picture with miles of mountains and blue sky above; the second was even better – twelve pairs of shoes standing on the ice.

After work, Gordon Forster, Morley McCallum, Brian MacKenzie, Steve Bullock, and I developed a routine of playing guitar and singing for about an hour before we went our separate ways. On occasion, a few other guys would join us as we learned and practiced songs like *For Loving' Me, Long River, In the Early Morning' Rain* by Gordon Lighfoot, *One Too Many Mornings* and others by Bob Dylan, *At My Door the Leaves are Fallin'*, and *Folsom Prison Blues* by Johnny Cash, along with a number of other songs by singer songwriters like Peter, Paul and Mary, Buffy St. Marie, and pop songs by the Byrds, the Beatles, and the Rolling Stones. Without knowing it, we were becoming well-rehearsed. I recall meeting up with Gordon and Brian at a party in Edmonton one winter, and after playing and singing a number of songs, some in an open tuning, a few guys at the party asked if we played professionally. We actually got paid for a few gigs that same winter, when Gordon and I joined up with Johnny McCallum (Morley's older brother) and played in folk clubs with names like Zorbas, The Outer Limits a Go-Go, and Giuseppe's Pizza Joint in Edmonton.

Wes Shennan, John McCallum & Gordon Forster,
Giuseppe's Pizza Joint, Edmonton, 1966

Wesley Shennan

Days off at the "ice" were even more enjoyable than the job. I skied on the glacier when I arrived during my second year in May. One evening, while we were skiing along with Jack Pugh's small dog from the Chalet, running and yelping beside us, he disappeared. We all stopped and side stepped back up the glacier to discover the dog had fallen through a rotten snow bridge and was wedged in a blue crevasse about twenty feet below us. I knew I didn't want to catch an edge and fall when I hit the really steep part at the toe, as I was looking right into the glacial lake, but I had no idea the snow was this rotten over the crevasses. Our routine of having the guys drop us off high on the moraine at the ticket office and driving down to the toe of the glacier to pick us up again came to an abrupt end. I was surprised the dog lived since hyperthermia sets in fast in a crevasse. At the same time, I was impressed by the expertise of the Park Warden, Hans, who extracted him in less than an hour. We all felt a little safer.

Another time near the beginning of my second year, I remember rising with the sun about 4 am with my girlfriend at the chalet staff residence (the Annex). We planned to go skiing at Parker Ridge about 10 miles south of the Icefields with two friends – Sheila Morris, who was around my age, and Helga, a gal of about 35. Although Helga was only 15 years older than me, she felt ancient, but she was a good skier. We hiked up Parker Ridge by kicking steps in the crusty snow with our ski boots, which took an hour and a half with the skies over our shoulder to get to the top, and then skied down above the tree line at first, then started cutting fast turns through the trees as we got closer to the bottom. Sheila and my girlfriend, Honya, weren't that experienced. They stayed near the bottom skiing in the trees.

Honya and I met at the Columbia Icefields Chalet on May 19, 1967. It was her summer job after attending university and she worked in the Chalet's upscale dining room as a waitress. When I first met her she called herself Helen, but when I learned she was

Russian and that her Russian name was Honya, I couldn't call her anything else – it sounded so exotic.

Although she was a second generation Canadian, her first language was Russian. Her parents were Doukhobors from the Kootenays in British Columbia. As paraphrased from the BC Archives, "Doukhobor" means "spirit wrestlers." They are Christian pacifists, a religious sect that dates back to the 1600s in Russia. The Doukhobor elders said "they wrestled with and for the Spirit of God" and their motto is "Toil and a Peaceful Life," which was reflected in their simple ways, communal living, and hard work. They came to Canada in 1899 and initially settled in Saskatchewan. After not agreeing to own individual plots of land because they lived communally, the sect broke up. Those staying in Saskatchewan and those moving to the Kootenays between 1908 to 1912, who continued to live communally with all of the land held in the name of their leader, Peter Verigin.

Primarily vegetarians, the sect prospered in British Columbia and developed commercial and industrial enterprises such as jam, jelly, and honey factories. Two separate groups evolved: the main group, who lived materialistic lives due to their prosperity, and a second, smaller group, The Sons of Freedom, who wanted to return to more traditional values and chose civil disobedience and violence to achieve their ideals. The Great Depression of the 1930s caused bankruptcy in the community as they had borrowed money for many of their enterprises. By the 1950s, the Sons of Freedom achieved notoriety in the newspapers by burning homes, schools, and gathering halls (not churches) of the main sect, bombing power lines, and marching nude to protest against materialism. I remembered these protests and ignorantly asked Honya, when I first met her, when she was going to take her clothes off. I was rebuked, given a terse history lesson, and told she was a member of the larger group of peaceful Orthodox Doukhobors.

Honya was my first love. My former romantic interludes were just that, they weren't love when compared to how I felt about this girl. We spent the summer of '67 together at the Icefields, in Banff, in Jasper, in Edmonton, and in places in between. At five feet two inches tall, natural honey blonde hair, blue eyes the same hue and intensity as the sky at the Icefields, a body as curvaceous as Marilyn Monroe, a heart that cried for others, and a mind that argued for righteousness, I was smitten.

When I was younger I used to read cheap poorly written novels about young lovers, especially the juicy parts, but at times, I felt like I was living in one of those fantasies. We would join Harold Gordon and Diane Hamel during work, sneak off to neck in a vacant snowmobile, and in the evening, drive to Jasper with Harold and Diane to drink at the Athabasca Hotel bar. The couple in the back seat always made out, being an hour drive to Jasper from the "ice." After we arrived, Harold would exhort all of us to sing his goofy little song:

> Well it's beer, beer, beer, that makes you want to cheer,
> on the lawn, on the lawn;
> Well it's beer, beer, beer, that makes you
> want to cheer, on the lawn of the chalet.

> Yes it's gin, gin, gin, that makes you want to grin, on the
> lawn, on the lawn;
> Yes, it's gin, gin, gin, that makes you want
> to grin on the lawn of the chalet.

> Well it's rum, rum, rum, that makes you want to come,
> on the lawn, on the lawn;
> Well it's rum, rum, rum, that makes you
> want to come on the lawn of the chalet.

Yes it's cold roast duck, that makes you want a sandwich, on the lawn, on the lawn;
Yes, it's cold roast duck that makes you want
a sandwich, on the lawn of the chalet.

It was a little dicey for me drawing all this attention, being the
only one under the age of 21. Everyone else, including Honya, was
21 or older, the legal drinking age in Alberta at the time. But there
was so much going on in this dance hall sized lair, like empty beer
glasses flying over our heads and smashing into the rock fire place,
as well as frequent fights, that I was never asked about my age.

Honya lived in the two-story staff residence, "The Annex,"
which was a smaller version of the chalet. Both buildings looked
like they were imported from Switzerland, with their red gable-end
steep roofs, wide eaves, many peaked dormers, thick dark brown
overlapping siding and rock foundations. Her room was on the
second floor overlooking the entrance through a dormer window.
One night we were having an impromptu party: I was playing
guitar and singing, her roommate Myrna, plus Lionel Rault and
Ted Bishop, who worked at the gas station, joined in, and we were
then joined by Harold Gordon and Bill Johnson, a guy who repaired
snowmobiles along with our main mechanic Ambrose. Bill was a
little taller than me, about six feet, had black wavy hair and looked
like he came from the Mediterranean. Bill and Harold had been
drinking too much and it was now time to challenge each other to
manly feats. Bill opened Honya's window, put his leg out and said
to Harold "let's go."

Harold hesitated, but Bill insisted, saying "you know I'm part
Indian, that's why I'm so wild. Come on, Harold, you can do it."

Bill slid down the roof and dropped two stories the ground. Not
to be out done, Harold did the same. We looked out the window
and they both seemed okay, rolling and laughing on the ground, but
what astounded me more than these feats were Bill's words. Even
when I drank too much, I didn't have the courage to admit I was

Wesley Shennan

part Indian. The only person who knew was Honya, and she promised not to tell anyone because, without knowing why, I had learned to be ashamed of my heritage. It was a teaching passed on through generations. I didn't learn about its conscious and unconscious power over me until years later.

The winter before I met Honya I was a ski lift operator at Lake Louise, located about 100 miles south of the Icefields in Banff National Park.

When Fred McDowell called from Lake Louise on a cold November morning in 1966 and said through his British accent "I've got your resume and I'd like you to come and work for me as a lift operator," the smile on my face wouldn't stop. I packed my skis, boots, and a navy blue metal chest containing all my belongings and packed them into the trunk of my light blue '59 Chevy coupe (the '55 Chevy had hidden rust and burnt oil, so I sold it and bought the '59 with a 283 V8 and dual glass pack mufflers).

Wes Shennan, Rossdale Flats, Edmonton, 1965

They closed the highway behind me around Red Deer on my way south from Edmonton. The snowflakes, like a never-ending flock of white butterflies fluttering at me, but swatted away at the last split second by the windshield wipers, started to blow across the road when the blizzard set in. I kept one eye on the ditch to the right and aimed the old Chevy between it where I thought the median ditch was on the left. At a constant 40 miles per hour, three bottles of alcohol in the gas tank so my carburettor and gas line didn't freeze up, and two brand new snow tires on the back, I started to relax. That is, until I hit snow drifts and passed two jack-knifed semis, one in the ditch on the right, and another in the ditch on the left, about 400 yards further down the road. By Airdrie the wind died down, and after a short break in Calgary, I continued on the snow-packed highway west to Banff and on to Lake Louise, where the snow was so high the road signs looked like they were sitting on the peak of the windrow.

Howard Shrigley, an ex-RCMP officer and outdoor manager for Lake Louise Lifts Limited, put me to work on the mogul cutter when I arrived. He was a really smooth skier, seemed to enjoy what he did, and had invented the mogul cutter. It was towed on metal skis behind a tracked vehicle called the *Nodwell,* driven skilfully by Bob Haney down the ski slopes, while I stood outside on the mogul cutter and hand operated a large toothed scoop. My job was to press down on top of the mogul and release the scooped snow by lifting the handle on the downhill side of the mogul. After a number of passes, the desired result was achieved – a groomed hill. The skiers, of course, would build up the moguls in three or four days, so we would start all over again. This predated snowboards, so consistent moguls were built up everywhere.

*Bob Haney operating the Nodwell, Wes Shennan on the
Mogul Cutter, Lake Louise, 1967. Photograph: Bruno Engler,
(1967) Ski Pictorial featuring ski area at Lake Louise*

Bob and I spent many hours grooming the slopes where I
learned he was a cowboy in the summer working for Bert Mickle
out of Temple Lodge on the backside of Lake Louise. One of his
summer jobs was to guide the Gorbys on horseback from Temple
Lodge, across Deception Pass, and on to Skoki Lodge. After talking
about horses and slightly exaggerating my limited riding experience on the Rez, Bert invited me to join them as a horse jingler on
roundup that fall. Bob said jinglers lose weight because they don't
have much time to eat as they are always chasing strays. Although
becoming even thinner didn't appeal to me, I, to this very day,
regret not being able to join them for a month on the trail rounding
up 200 horses in the Rockies and herding them past the foothills
and on to the prairie for the winter.

I was thankful Bob was a skilful driver. Once, while we were
cutting moguls on the ski out from Temple Lodge on the backside of
the mountain, down to the parking lot at the bottom of the Sedan Lift
on the Whitehorn side of the mountain, my scoop hit a tree root that
jerked the handle suddenly upward, with me hanging on. I flew and

landed between the *Nodwell* and the mogul cutter. Bob stopped the *Nodwell* before the mogul cutter ran over me. We both had a good laugh, probably not realizing how dangerous it really was.

After working with Bob for a couple of months, I became the main operator of the Larch hill *Poma Lift* on the back side of Lake Louise next to Temple Lodge until I left in early May. The lift was invented by a French guy named Jean Pomagalski and consisted of a disk about the size of a Frisbee attached to a telescoping pole released onto a fast moving cable. After you placed the pole between your legs and the operator pulled the release, you were immediately jerked into action as the disk pulled you up the mountain. Seeing round disks tucked firmly into the buttocks of girls in tight ski pants made standing in the snow all day a little easier.

I liked operating the *Poma Lift*. After checking the oil, I started the large six cylinder *Cummins* diesel every morning by pulling a compression release lever before cranking it over. When it was minus 25. the old *Cummins* turned over a few more times, but it always started. As soon as it kicked in, I let go of the compression release lever and black smoke poured out of the exhaust pipe poking out of the wall of the lift shack. The engine warmed up in about five minutes and that's when I engaged the clutch to turn the big bull wheel outside. The bull wheel sent the cable up and down the mountain, and as soon as the lift was running, I quickly put on my skies, grabbed a *Poma* pole, stuffed it between my legs and hit the release.

On my way up on the inspection run, I was supposed to check the cable guide wheels (we called them sheaves) at each tower. When I reached the top of the lift, I hit the emergency shut-off. Of course, I was then burdened with skiing all the way down Larch hill to start the *Cummins* again. Sometimes there were early skiers waiting when I arrived at the lift shack. They had just watched me ski down the hill without another soul in sight, often through a foot of fresh powder in the bright sunshine. It was burdensome, alright. I usually had other jobs at the end of the day I also enjoyed, but not quite as much as skiing after my inspection. They involved replacing the springs inside the *Poma* poles so that they would telescope properly, and driving new rivets into the sleeves at the top of the poles, designed to grab the fast moving cable when the operator hit the release.

Shortly after becoming the operator of the Larch hill *poma*, Howard skied over and said "shut 'er down. You have to come 'n help us, a guy's buried in an avalanche."

I put on my skies, skied down the beginner hill behind Temple Lodge, and skated over to the Ptarmigan Chair Lift. There were three guys skiing out of bounds west of the Ptarmigan chair: a Swiss Car mechanic from Banff who was learning to ski powder, Bernie Schiesser, a ski instructor and mountaineer from Golden B.C., and Fritz, a ski instructor from Mount Norquay. When the avalanche came down, the Swiss mechanic was the highest on the slope, and although he fell over, the avalanche was mostly downhill from him. Bernie was the farthest down the slope and buried to the waist. He said the snow felt like concrete packed around his legs. Fritz was in the middle and completely buried. Don Mickle, Bert's son, new to the Warden Service and on duty that day, organized us to find Fritz. Ski patrollers, lift operators, instructors, people from Temple lodge, and a few others (about 20 of us), lined up across the avalanche with slalom poles in our hands. Don told us to probe the snow, move down the slope in a straight continuous line, and keep probing until we found Fritz. There weren't enough of us to cover the entire width of the avalanche so we started to branch out on our own.

The search seemed to take forever. I think it was at least half an hour before another guy and I noticed our slalom poles didn't go into the avalanche as far as usual because we hit something. It was Fritz. The ski patrollers dug him out quickly and a red haired patroller immediately gave him mouth to mouth resuscitation. Fritz looked like he was breathing, but it was only the red head's air coming out of him every time the patroller stopped to take another breath. The ski patroller was exhausted after 20 solid minutes and

I was amazed he was able to maintain the resuscitation for so long. Unfortunately, Fritz was probably dead before we dug him out. He was in his mid-30's, originally from Switzerland, and an instructor at Mount Norquay above Banff town site. He came to Lake Louise for a day of fresh powder. We tried to make ourselves feel better by saying "well at least he died doing what he loved," but looking at Fritz's blue lifeless face silently reminded me of my friend's two brothers who were killed in a car accident just a few years earlier. Death is so final, yet so relentless for those of us left. I was surprised the RCMP didn't interview me. Although we talked about it a little, after a few months, Fritz's death wasn't mentioned anymore.

When I first arrived at Lake Louise my skiing skills were pretty basic compared to the guys who already worked there. I immediately enrolled in my one and only ski lesson from a guy named Heinz. Mike Wiegele, an Austrian, ran the ski school at that time, and the majority of the instructors were from Austria. I asked Heinz how long he worked for Mike and he said he just started before Christmas, but because he was studying in Austria, he was returning home after Christmas. I got to know a few other instructors, like Wolfgang Ehmann and his buddy Hubert. They, along with Mike, lived in a log cabin near ours behind the Post Hotel. Bearded Bernie, Mike's ski technician and a folk singer in the style of Peter, Paul and Mary, said Wolfgang's left knee looked like a bag full of marbles. Wolfgang was in his early twenties, but his racing career came to an abrupt end when his *Marker Long Thong* made sure his knee twisted when he fell during a downhill race on the Hannekahn in the Austrian Alps. A few years later, I was saddened to learn Wolfgang died in a helicopter crash while powder skiing in the Bugaboos.

Heinz taught me the check, plant, and jump method of parallel skiing. We would ski across the fall line, allow the tails of our skis to slide slightly downhill, plant our downhill pole, then jump by putting weight on our shovels and bringing the tails back up to continue in a straight line across the hill. After practicing this back and forth across the fall line, which included stopping and kick turns, Heinz said it was time to jump right around the pole. Instead of jumping and bringing our skis back to continue across the fall line, we were supposed to maintain weight on our shovels and rotate around our pole until we were facing the opposite direction on the fall line. He said it was often easier when we could use a little mogul by checking (allowing our tails to slide slightly downhill), planting our pole on top, and turning on the downhill side of the mogul. Heinz's lesson was serious and he wasn't kidding when he said we couldn't smoke, not even when we were riding the lift. After practicing and practicing by skiing over the mountain every morning to the Larch Hill lift next to Temple Lodge, skiing on my inspection run after I opened the *Poma Lift* every day, and skiing on all of my days off, I was manoeuvring through the black diamond moguls confidently in about two months. However, it wasn't until spring when I felt I could really fly.

I remember tearing over the top of the steep Ptarmigan run one bright sunny April morning on my day off, when I caught up to one of Mike's few female instructors. I don't remember her name, but I do know we kind of liked each other. We would chat and say things like "what's the colour of those eyes behind the sunglasses?" whenever she got onto my *Poma Lift* on Larch hill. This particular morning, she was giving an expert lesson, teaching a guy to ski moguls. I noticed, with some interest, his expensive skin-tight black ski racing pants with a wide white stripe down the outside of both legs, a matching black ski jacket with subtle white trim, black and white toque and gloves, sunglasses with white trim, new black *Lange* buckle boots, and skiing on a pair of brand new black *Head Slalom Competitions* with the latest *Look/Nevada* step-in bindings.

The instructor and I smiled and exchanged our usual flirty remarks, which seemed to incense this guy. He looked me up and down with disgust, dressed in my normal lift operator gear: blue jeans with beige knee high canvas gaiters covering my *Tyrol* lace-up boots, older *Head Masters* with a *Marker/Lift* front-throw binding, a black and white tweed sweater my mom knitted for me, longish black curly hair blowing in the breeze, wrap-around sun glasses, and an exceptionally dark tan, hinting to my First Nation heritage. The guy sneered, pushed off in a huff, and skied his best through the moguls. The instructor and I smiled at each other, and with a slight chuckle, pushed off at the same time. We caught up to this guy, who was now standing on a mogul and breathing hard after falling. She stopped and I kept going. I heard her say something to him like, "this is what I want you to do," as I entered my next jump turn and continued gaining speed through the moguls until I was quickly out of sight.

My buddies from Edmonton visited in January and returned in February. Terry Harris and Grant Cameron stayed with me in log cabin for a while (until Fred McDowell sent us a letter about "harbouring friends"), but they persevered, hung around long enough, sometimes sleeping in the women's can at the Sedan Lift which was nicer than the men's, and were eventually hired in March. With Gerry Shea and Gordon Harper's frequent visits, we spent a very fast spring skiing every run at Lake Louise. Brian could never make it because he was saving his money to visit his girlfriend Donna Lauredson in Alaska and go skiing at Mount Alyeska. I remember starting at the top of Larch Hill on a spring afternoon, putting my skis together and heading for the ski out. The only turns I made were the ones I needed to because the road turned. I skied five miles to the Sedan Lift parking lot in a little less than 15 minutes. This was fairly fast since much of the ski out was flat and you had to skate like mad to make that kind of time. Grant liked to pick up speed and finish his run with an impressive jump next to the lift at the bottom of Larch Hill, but on a day near the end of the season in May, there was a fellow standing right where he normally landed. Grant broke his ankle, which didn't allow him to return to the Columbia Icefields that summer for his third year.

I lived with three guys in log cabin number four, next to the Pipestone River behind the Post Hotel. By spring, we started saying, "there's a cabin at party four!" When I first arrived at Lake Louise, I was living with Rudy Junker, an outstanding skier from Switzerland who left near the end of the season to work as a carpenter in northern British Columbia and visited me later that summer at the Icefields, Roger Hamilton, a guy from Calgary who would bring girls home and make love to them after we were all "asleep," and Don Fowler from a small town in BC, who at 26 already had a nine year old daughter, Valerie. I didn't believe him until he showed me her birthday card. By March, Roger had left for the Barbados to scuba dive and Don Fowler went back to Banff after a disagreement with Howard Shrigley. Jack Schiesser, Bernie's younger brother, moved into the corner bed where Don was and Grant took Roger's old bed next to the door. Fred McDowell, the guy who hired me, and head man on the hill for Lake Louise Lifts Limited, was an Englishman who lived with his family in a two-storey log home between our cabin and the Post Hotel. Unfortunately, Fred could not relate to people and seemed to have only a vague idea of operating an efficient ski resort. He lost our respect, including Howard's, and a drunk Jack Schiesser would stagger outside at night and yell "Hey McDowell, you couldn't operate a fucking chicken coop!" We would run outside, drag him in, saying "for Christ's sake Jack, shut up."

Sven Christianson, an alcoholic Dane and outdoor mechanic, who often joined, drank with us and would say, "Ho, ho, sit Jack" (sit meaning shit). If there were any concerns about this time in my life, I'd have to say it was excessive drinking.

There was a South African nurse, Pippa, who took the winter off and worked on the ski hill. After she saw me take a drink of water in the morning while working on the lift and immediately get high from the excessive amount of scotch left in my system from the night before, she said "I pity your poor liver." That comment brought me instant chills. I was almost hit by a swinging *poma* disk. I remembered Uncle Vic had died of cirrhosis of the liver just a few years earlier. It seems we all go through a rite of passage, as most of us don't have a ceremony recognizing manhood like the Jewish Bar Mitzvah or a First Nation Vision Quest. Our ceremony often involves being rebellious, consuming excessive drink, drugs, and womanizing during the late teens or early twenties. I am thankful the drug scene was just beginning to happen at this time and was not a big part of our lives. My friends were experimenting with marijuana, and Doug Smith, another guitar playing and singing buddy on the ski hill, wrote a long treatise describing his experience with LSD, but drugs like that were just coming on the scene.

I drank in excess for about two years, but meeting Honya made a big change in my life-style. My new responsibilities soon steered me away from becoming an alcoholic and away from the so-called recreational drugs that became more prevalent by the late '60s.

After I finished working at Lake Louise in May, I came back to Edmonton for a two-week period before travelling to the Icefields for my second year. A guy my dad worked with rebuilt the 283 V8 in my '59 Chevy, which left me without a car for about two weeks. During the day, I played guitar and practiced almost eight hours a day, learning the revolving thumb (Merle Travis) style of folk finger picking. I listened to the album *Lightfoot!* over and over and tried to sound like Red Shea, Gordon Lighfoot's guitar player. In the evenings, I spent a lot of time with my favourite group of girls, especially Joan Ullman. Since I didn't have a car, I telephoned Joanie and wondered if she would like to go on a reverse date. She would have to pick me up after supper in her little burgundy Mini.

"Just be sure you are standing at the door and ready to go as soon as I get there," she said.

Joanie lived in east Edmonton. It took about 20 minutes before she drove into the yard in front of the block. I spent many evenings with her during those two weeks and I could feel myself becoming closer and closer to her. Some nights we held hands and walked, without saying too much, through the large gardens south of the

Alberta Legislature building. Other times we went for pizza, where Terry Harris and Gordon Harper worked, and sat and talked while we ate our free pizza. We went dancing one night and I remember admiring her straight, shiny, almost waist-length dark brown hair as it swayed back and forth over her slim fitting brown blouse tucked into a pair of guy's tight blue jeans. We danced "the walk," which was something like a jive step. I liked holding her close to me and spinning her around. Her coy expression made me feel serious and protective. I spent a weekend with Joanie at Mameo Beach the spring before but we weren't alone. Inge Stauning, Linda Hadley, Heather Cochrane, and Joanie rented a cabin for the long weekend in May, and invited me, Terry, Brian, Grant, and Gordon to join them – a kind of group date. We drank lots, sang songs (I remember Grant and I doing a drunken *House of the Rising Sun* duet more than once), danced every night to the Nomads until the sun came up and slept as couples. I honestly don't think anyone had serious sex beyond necking and a little groping. It felt like we were preserving our innocence, or something, and didn't want to venture off into the deeper feelings and emotions that were tied to more serious sex.

Inge and Linda had moved from home and were renting in one of Edmonton's few high rises, which was recently constructed in the flats below McKay Avenue on 104th Street when I returned from Lake Louise that spring. I think Inge's parents were Danish, which explained her almost waist-length straight naturally blonde hair and cheery fine features which lit up when she looked at me. She couldn't believe the tan I had when I showed up at her door. She invited me in and we drank tea one evening and talked about the Rockies and what it was like skiing every day for five months.

Another night when Inge was out I visited with Linda. She was a natural model. I remember asking her if she was interested in becoming one. She was at least 5'10" tall, very thin but still curvy, and carried herself in a confident manner. I think her light brown hair had some natural curl to it, or else she just couldn't be bothered ironing her hair on an ironing board like so many girls did at the time. Gordon nicked named her "jump ball" after the tall centres who jump for the ball in basketball games. She told me she couldn't become a model because her teeth were too crooked. Adults with braces certainly weren't common in the '60s, so neither of us even thought about straightening her teeth with braces.

When we had our group date at Mameo Beach, Joanie was my partner, but when it came time to end the weekend and drive home, Inge and Linda ended up coming with me. The three of us were driving by some road construction workers and they couldn't believe I had two beautiful girls sitting right beside me on the Chevy's front bench seat. In some ways, neither could I, feeling an easy, comforting friendship with these ladies. I enjoyed being with them both and didn't feel stressed at all. I could be open and honest. I didn't have sisters, so maybe it was almost a sibling-type relationship.

It was around this time when Inge and Linda had a party and someone showed up with marijuana. Joanie and I weren't there, but you would think the reporters were, with headlines like "Edmonton's first pot bust!" saying "you could smell the sweet pungent odour all the way down the hall." I felt sorry for the girls. They had to be bailed out of jail by their parents.

When I told my dad, he said to me "if you are dumb enough to end up in jail, you can damn well stay there." I knew he meant it. That summer I talked briefly to Inge and Linda at a dance in Jasper and introduced them to Honya. I think that was the last time I saw my two "sisters." The following summer, Honya and I were waiting at the street corner on a hot summer day in Edmonton when I noticed the familiar locks of straight dark brown shiny hair right in front of me. Joanie was wearing a short white slim-fitting print summer dress. I felt she knew I was there, but didn't turn around. It was the last time I remember seeing her.

Wesley Shennan

5. TEACHINGS, TRAINS AND GHOSTS

MY LIFE BEGAN IN A CRIB AROUND THE age of three, or so it seems. Before that, I'm now not sure where I was. Apparently, I was born on October 18, 1946 in Edmonton, named Wesley Maurice Shennan, have genes that go back to Mohawks from Kahnawake, Quebec, and Huguenots from France, but I don't remember that. So, I'll start in that crib sometime in 1949.

Our first suite in "The Block" was a bachelor on the top north east corner of the old three story building. It was jammed with the bedroom, kitchen and living room furniture my dad got for landing on the beach at Normandy, June 16, 1944, ten days after D-Day during the Second World War. Years later, dad told me a guy wanted 20 bucks under the table so that he could be put on the veteran's housing list, but I told him "to stuff it up his ass." Knowing my dad, the guy was probably expecting an upper cut to his lower jaw to knock him out, but no matter how right my dad was, all we ended up with was a room in an old building with too much furniture.

Mom, new to city life at 25, having been born Christina Bernadette Callihoo at Villeneuve, May 29, 1924, busied herself making curtains, waxing the maple hardwood floor, dusting the dark brown mahogany vanity and bedroom chest of drawers, and bed stead. She rearranged the overstuffed dark blue paisley couch and two matching chairs, putting the dishes and cutlery in the light brown birch hutch with red trim, and polished the matching kitchen table and four chairs. For a few years, we didn't own a refrigerator, so mom would keep milk and butter outside on the window sill. Every once in a while the milk would freeze in the winter, the round cardboard insert sitting on top of a thick finger of frozen milk that pushed itself up through the open mouth of the glass milk bottle.

"No, don't touch that again!" Were mom's stern words when she told me not to pull her prized crystal lamp off the vanity. I remember doing it the day before by reaching though the bars of my light brown wooden crib, pulling the white crocheted doily and watching the lamp and bulb smash on the hardwood floor—a square crystal leg breaking off and rolling to the door like a dye in a game of chance. This created quite a flurry of dust pans, brooms, and harsh words while the soft classical music played from the dark brown mahogany radio/record player and the sun painted friendly yellow lines across the maple floor. I don't remember crying, so I guess mom had just the right balance of sternness for me to learn.

Mom married dad, William Shennan (born on August 4, 1921, Edmonton) in 1946. They lived in two other places in Edmonton before moving to "The Block" in 1947. Dad worked at a number of jobs after his discharge from the army as a motorcycle dispatch rider. When he worked in the produce department at the Hudson's Bay, he told me, he couldn't stand the little old ladies who would pinch every tomato until they were all bruised. Shortly after that job, he became a truck driver for the provincial government, delivering everything from furniture to cement mixers throughout the province – a more solitary job that suited his personality a lot better and which he kept until retirement at age 58.

My crib was wedged between Mom and Dad's bed and the vanity. We lived in that bachelor suite where I had a roll away cot after a while, until we moved to a three room suite down the hall when I was five. Living that close for those years resulted in sharing experiences that wouldn't normally be shared if we had slept in separate rooms. After hearing repeated muted sighs of ecstasy, it became a regular part of my life and unbeknownst to them I would actually listen for it after a while. I had an imaginary friend, Blue, who became my lover and taught me loving was natural, that it was okay and not mysterious or taboo. When I recall these times, it seems society today is still mired in Victorian values to some degree, with loving kept behind closed bedroom doors and children kept distant from it until they are "old enough to understand." But what age is "old enough to understand?" I lived beside loving from infancy until age five and I wonder how many rooms and doors there were in the little stone houses where granddad grew up in Kirkcudbright, Scotland in the late 1800s. I know for sure there were no rooms or doors in the tepee when mom attended a Sundance as a kid in Hobbema in 1930, or in the open upstairs bedroom in the log house on the Rez. Perhaps the natural learning that happens when we live close has only been removed from our lives recently. As Thomas Moore says in *The Soul of Sex*, our sex-obsessed life only looks on the surface. He goes on to say that sex is more closely related to the soul. When dealt with thoughtfully, the whole interior cosmos comes to the foreground. With this in mind, perhaps teaching sex is much more complex than simply taking about the "birds and the bees" when you think a child is "old enough." Maybe this teaching could start more easily and naturally at a much younger age. When older, a child who grew up in the same room as his parents instinctively senses the interior completeness and depth of it all. To some degree, this is what I think happened to me. I always liked girls and couldn't be close enough to them. I liked talking with them and, when I was in my teens, enjoyed looking at the nudes in *Playboy* magazine and reading about having sex as it was described in cheap corner store novels. Still, I never felt compelled to bed every chick that crossed my path and carve a notch on my bed post for every conquest, like some of my friends did. I feel the same today. All the lovers I have ever had in my life can be counted on one hand.

Aunt Helen, my Dad's sister, visited us often in that little bachelor suite. I remember a very special visit when I was four. The late August sun couldn't penetrate the coolness of that day. Leaves from the big poplar trees in the playground were turning their familiar bright yellow; some were falling. Helen (I didn't call her Aunt or Auntie), wore her forest green wool coat with covered buttons. It matched her reddish hair and freckles.

"I want you to remember this, Wesley. You can tell your Grandchildren you were part of history."

I can remember saying something like "Helen, I don't have Grandchildren. I'm only four."

"I know sweetheart, but someday you may be a Grandfather and you can tell them."

"Tell them what?"

"Oh, I'm just going to take you there. You'll see."

We walked hand-in-hand up 97th Avenue, under the silver steel arch of the Seventh Street Bridge crossing above our heads to the Alberta Legislature. We passed the corner restaurant with the thick chrome pedestal stools and on to 109th. Street.

I remember that restaurant clearly. A few years later, Brian MacKenzie and I had just finished delivering the **Edmonton Journal** when we stopped in for a milkshake and talked to the owner. He must have had a stroke or something because his face had a permanent sneer, but his eyes seemed kind enough. As his wife in a white apron looked on from the kitchen, he bragged about his only son who attended McKay a few years earlier than Brian and I. He even showed us his son's faded red school sweater with a few small yellow crests of merit sewn on it. I think that was the only time I was ever in that restaurant. It looked so inviting with its curved wall entrance and black trimmed windows, but I couldn't get past the sneer and didn't really want to come back and stay, not even for one of those great tasting vanilla milk shakes.

Helen and I crossed 109th Street and waited on the curb. The streetcar creaked quietly then stopped. We had to walk into the street to get on because the streetcar couldn't pull up to the curb like a bus. We continued toward the High Level Bridge by crossing to the track on the opposite side.

Helen allowed me to stand on the tan leather seat, which was something my Dad would never let me to do. I held onto the varnished wooded sill, pressed my face to the rattley window and looked down. I saw absolutely nothing, except the clear North Saskatchewan River flowing below me. I loved it. I was one of those kids who would later never get enough of circus rides, so this was just pure exhilaration.

On September 2, 1951 the streetcars of the Edmonton Radial Railway made their final trips. Helen knew this and wanted to make sure I would remember riding on it before Edmonton's streetcars disappeared into the history books. The electric railway had become famous back then, as the High Level Bridge crossing at 152 feet above the river was the highest in the world. Inaugurated in 1913, it linked Edmonton to the then-separate community of Strathcona.

The High Level Bridge was originally designed for trains, streetcars, vehicles, and pedestrians. The top deck had three sets of tracks. The centre was for the Canadian Pacific steam locomotives and the two outer tracks on the very edge were for the streetcars. After the streetcars were abandoned, there were tracks left downtown and on Whyte Avenue. I can remember my Dad smirking and manoeuvring our 1948 two-tone green Chevrolet coupe on those rails so we could all enjoy a smoother ride.

I was still about four when I had my first encountered another type of train.

I didn't spend all my four-year-old life in "The Block," and sometimes I would visit Gramma, Grampa and my aunt Betty, who was more like my sister than an auntie. They lived on "the farm" and it was a short train ride northwest of Edmonton to Villeneuve.

After spending a weekend on "the farm," it was time to go home.

"Come on, my man. Put your shoes on," Gramma demanded.

"Why?"

"We're taking you back to Mommy's."

After Gramma locked the main door, a long straight spring creaked and pulled the wooden green screen door closed, while a small spring-loaded mouth with rollers for teeth instantly snapped the door into its jamb. Betty, Gramma, and I stood on the front landing while grampa backed the bustle-back Mercury out of the garage. The tires crackled on the black cinder driveway like caramel popcorn.

Gramma slid into the front seat while Betty and I crammed into the back through the maroon suicide doors. Grampa thumped the heavy cream can into the trunk. I remember the rumble of the engine, a V8 flathead, soothing me as we turned out of the drive-way and raised a little summer dust. We stopped at the station by Villeneuve's three grain elevators. Everyone got out.

"Come and put your ear down here," Betty said as she pointed and bent down beside the tracks.

The warm steel felt comforting next to my ear, but I didn't hear anything on the shiny surface except for a faint scratching sound. Then way off in the distance, where the rails met, I saw black smoke. I stood up and ran to the platform as the black smoke seemed to get bigger and bigger really fast.

"Put your thumb and finger up to your eye and look at the smoke that way, isn't it small?" Betty asked, "See, it's not even as big as your eye!"

It was small, but growing way too fast. It was coming to get me. I saw a face with puffy black cheeks, a one-eyed light in the middle, black smoke pouring from the top and white smoke from the sides. It filled my whole body, bigger and bigger, and I could hear it panting in short choppy breaths—*hawah-hawah-hawah-hawah-hawah-hawah*—getting louder and louder.

The one-eyed face suddenly poured white smoke straight up really fast and screamed. As it passed the level crossing about half a mile away, it sounded mad and sad at the same time.

I heard another scream – it was my own. I started to sob. "It's going to get me!"

Betty looked at me with her best sad eyes, but I knew deep down she was laughing. She set me up.

Gramma took my hand. "Come on, my man. We'll wait inside."

The windows in the waiting room shook and the panting was louder and louder and slower and slower. Wiping away my tears, I heard a bell, which sounded friendly, but a shadow appeared. A screaming, hissing big black snake coming to eat me was right outside the window.

In 1950, you couldn't go far in Alberta before running into railway tracks and grain elevators. The local lines have mostly been abandoned now, but back then, railroads crisscrossed the southern half of the province like the string inside a baseball. If you had to get somewhere in Alberta, you often went by steam loco-motive. With fewer highways, even little hamlets like Villeneuve on the Michel Reserve grew because of the railway. Transporting pas-sengers and freight, like Grampa's cream, made these little places swarm like a kicked-in ant hill whenever the screaming, hissing big black snake arrived.

They took me back home to "The Block." With its high plaster ceilings, it always felt lonely and cold, compared to the warm low wooden ceiling forming the second floor of the log house on "the farm."

A few nights after I arrived, dad was playing cards with our neighbour Cliff Evans. "Okay Wesley, time for bed," dad would say.

I opened the door of the suite. The dimly lit hall was quiet – nobody there. The neighbours weren't using the common bathroom – nobody there. I ran into the hall and around the corner into the bathroom.

The small pale green cubicle felt safe. The walls were close. No one could sneak up on me. I could sit here forever. *You can't sit here all night,* I thought. *Mom will wonder what's taking so long. Who's there? I don't want to leave, but I have to leave; I know Mom will come looking for me and say I'm taking too long. But I don't want leave. Maybe I can pee some more. I did, now what? You have to leave. Okay, okay.*

The cubicle door was open to the shadows. I wanted to run like mad back to our suite like I did every night, but tonight it was different. I listened. *Don't run, look behind you,* I thought to myself. *What was that breath behind me every night? Okay, you're in the hall now, look. I can't. Don't you want to know? Yes, but I'm scared. Look behind you.*

I turned and there he was—a man, but smaller than me. His white gleaming teeth against his dark skin grinned. But his grin didn't reach his eyes. They had no love, no feeling. He just stared. I froze momentarily. Then I howled. I turned and ran through the door of our apartment, burying my head in Mom and Dad's bed sobbing and shuddering.

Mom and Dad were stunned in disbelief. Cliff Evans immediately rushed out of our apartment. "I'll get him for you, Wesley!"

After that, my fear of the bathroom seemed to evaporate. I didn't feel afraid to go to the bathroom any more. Although I never met him again, as an adult I still believe he was there.

"The Block" was located very near the original site of Fort Edmonton when it was first constructed in the early 1800s. Since then, there have been many official and unofficial archaeological discoveries. One I remember in particular was the unearthing of skeletons during the expansion of the Rossdale Water Treatment Plant in the '60s. I sometimes wonder: *was the block built on a spirit who met an untimely death? Was this a distant relative teaching me about the spirit world?*

Mom and dad lived in the block until dad retired and they moved to British Columbia in 1982. While they were living there, mom came home from work one day and opened a Christmas Card from my Auntie Jean. Inside was a cute picture of my cousin Paulette. Mom put the card and picture on the coffee table. When dad came home she was making supper,

"Have a look at the cute picture of Paulette in the Christmas Card," She said.

Dad went into the living room "There's no picture of Paulette."

They searched and searched. They never did find her picture. Another time, dad was sorting his amateur coin collection on the kitchen table when a coin dropped on the floor and rolled toward the kitchen sink. He left his chair, got down on his knees to pick up the coin and it wasn't there. A few years later they moved to B.C. "Now I'm gonna find that coin because the whole kitchen is empty," He said. He never found it.

The caretaker of "The Block," Lucie Evans, who still lives there at the time of this writing, sent a poem to my Dad for his eightieth birthday:

The Soul of a Building, By Lucie Evans

The old brick building groans with every movement.
Inside, there is a musty aging scent.
The nights are quiet in the hollow empty halls.
Yet there are strange sounds pervading the walls.
It clings to you, this empty silence.
Perhaps there was a time of violence.
Somehow, I felt strange arms around me and saw no one.
Who lingers there to make their presence known?
Were they always alone?
It is time to leave this lonely place of time and decay.
Forgotten by all who pass by each day.

6. A WORLD TILTED 180 DEGREES

MOM SAID SHE CRIED WHEN SHE SENT ME off for my first day of school at Donald Ross Elementary. "My baby was growing up," she told me years later. To be honest, I don't even remember that first day. What I do remember about that first year of school was calmness and tranquillity. I'd come home for lunch and mom would be there with CKUA or CJCA on the radio and she'd ask "how was your morning?" After school, she'd be peeling potatoes for supper or sewing, saying I could play outside until dad came home.

During the summer mom got a job as a seamstress at the Snowflake Laundry. When I entered grade two, the axis of my little world tilted 180 degrees. Mom and dad were off to work two hours before I went to school, so I ate breakfast alone. Dad would try to meet me for lunch (which he managed most days, but he had to work out of town sometimes since he drove a truck for the Alberta Government) and I was on my own after school until around 5:30 when mom and dad came home. I couldn't tell time during the first few months of grade two, so I'd place my books near the door in the morning, walk into the next room, and take painstakingly slow steps toward them to kill a few hours before going to school (mom showed me where the hands on the clock would be for school time).

Other days, I'd call on my buddy Jim Branter so early in the morning I'd wake up his whole household. Around 12:30 after lunch, I'd run to the window and listen to dad's truck pull away, a large six cylinder engine in a three-ton GMC truck. I'd really concentrate on the sound gaps between the pistons firing, which was something like listening to the radio and quickly turning the volume up and down. After a while you hear a series of short silent gaps with music chopped in the background (I play this game today, on occasion, and still hear the noise of an engine in the distance—*ohwm, ohwm, ohwm,* with silence having the same intensity as the combustion). I was evolving from the carefree extrovert in grade one to a withdrawn, grade two introvert, largely because I was left on my own and had no one to talk to without brothers or sisters at home. I withdrew to an inner world of imagination, thought, and concentration. Without knowing it, I think I was trying to get the love of my parents by falling into a rebellious attitude and life-style.

The Edmonton Police department paid attention to my rebellion, and on more than one occasion, they'd come to the school and ask about me. "Is there a Wesley Shennan here?" I couldn't believe it when I saw the policemen standing at the back of the room the first time, in their dark navy blue uniforms. *I don't remember anyone seeing us – how could they possibly know today that Ralph Keiser, Phillip Lovell, Patrick Vandergaag, and I pulled shingles off the old community hall—that was yesterday!* I thought to myself.

The policemen took us into the Principal's office and when they asked Ralph how many shingles he pulled off. "About two," he said.

They asked Phillip next and he said the same thing. I was third. My dad taught me to always tell the truth, so I thought for a while and said "I pulled off about ten shingles."

Last was Patrick and a big smile came over his face. He wasn't to be outdone and when they asked him how many shingles he pulled off, he proudly said "I pulled off twenty."

The cops said we would be entered in their "black book," and if we kept breaking the law, the next step was reform school. They asked us to write our names down.

"I can't write," I said. They probably thought I didn't want my name recorded, but I was just telling the truth again. I could print my name, but I was just learning how to write.

"You are in grade two and you can't write?" the policeman asked.

I scribbled something that looked like writing, left the principal's office, and went back to class. *Don't they know we're learning to write? Why didn't they let me print my name?* I thought.

The next police visit was a little more serious. Hans January, Phillip Lovell, and I broke an upstairs back window in a house, smashed a number of light bulbs, and threw a box of wooden matches into the furnace in the basement. We thought it was an abandoned house, but a family was moving in that day. The cops even came to the block in the evening and told our parents what we did. I think Phillip and I ended up paying for some of the damage out of our allowance and were grounded for a couple of weeks. I don't think they ever talked to Hans.

The summer after grade two, I caught scarlet fever. Mom said I asked her to straighten pictures on the wall that weren't there because I was delirious for three days. I remember vomiting so often I thought dying would help me escape the relentless feeling of sickness. I had visions of three large puffy grey balls rolling at me, feeding me like a bad meal, and making my body expand until I filled the room, my face touching the ceiling. The scarlet fever lasted for about a month. After a second month of quarantine as Dr. Lobsinger ordered (doctors made home visits in those days), I was literally climbing the walls to get outside.

When I entered grade three that fall I continued on my rebellious path and decided to quit. *What does school matter? I don't really care*, I would ask myself. Mrs. Mills was my grade three teacher and I remember purposely ignoring her lessons. School didn't matter anymore and, although my report cards weren't great, I wasn't failing. But the final one, of course, was different. *Oh God no, I've failed!* I thought. *You're stupid! You're a loser!*

Even though I kind of planned it and, although two guys failed along with me – my buddy Gilbert Todd and Eugene Kliparchuk, I was planning to quit not fail. I remember going to Wings Grocery to pick up some empty cardboard boxes for our trip to Yellowstone

National Park after school closed for that summer, and Gary Schurman, my buddy Pete's older brother, said "you still get to go on holidays when you failed; shouldn't they make you stay home?"

I kind of agreed with him, but at the same time I was glad mom and dad made me feel that failing wasn't as big a setback as I thought it was. I could do better next year. I was also happy to leave the flats and escape some of my self-condemnation, guilt, and the peer pressure for a while.

Seated L to R: Richard Pacquin, Judy Oman, Irma, Patrick Vandergaag; Front Row, L to R: Eugene Kliparchuk, Ken Leaderer, Larry Danielson, Kenny Hatt, Wayne Dodds, Wesley Shennan, Gilbert Todd, Ken Wilkes; Second Row L to R: Gail Vandergaag, Patricia, Gay Campbell, April?, Evonne, Audrey Vandomsolaar; Erica, Edith; Back Row, L to R: Donny McLeod, Richard Seagull, Russell Monk, Ellis Smith, Richard Rutar, Ramsey Twins, Richard Jolen and Mrs. Mills, Grades three and four, Donald Ross Elementary School, Edmonton, Alberta, 1954, Photograph by Jake Van Loon, 9532 -100ᵗʰ Street, Edmonton, Alberta

For about four or five summers in a row in elementary through junior high, I would go to Aunt Betty and Uncle Les's farm for my vacation in southern Alberta. It was near Milk River, dusty little town of 800 on the flat prairie with five grain elevators, a Chinese restaurant, a hotel, a beer parlour, and few farm equipment dealers 50 miles south of Lethbridge (the regional capital of 30,000) and about 10 miles from the "line," to the United States.

The farm was located halfway between Milk River and the border town of Sweetgrass, Montana. Les taught me to drive a *John Deere 730* tractor towing a hydraulically operated chisel plough. My first job was summer fallow and the biggest thrill was waving to the neighbours who were driving by on the country road while I churned up the dust and easily rounded the corners with the tractor's power steering. I also learned to tow the binder with Les on board and he said my corners were better than the Thompson brothers across the road because I really paid attention to when to turn (you could tell how good the corners were by the number of oats left standing on the corners when you were finished).

A binder's job is to cut the grain, tie a single sheaf around the middle with binder twine, and after dropping six sheaves in a pile (which was Les's job operating the binder), we would walk around the whole field stooking the sheaves. When we were done stooking, there were small pyramids of drying sheaves everywhere.

That is as far as I got before going back to school at harvest time. One Saturday dad took me to the "north quarter" where granddad lived near the end of his life north of Spruce Grove. We watched as the dried stooks were loaded onto wagons pulled by tractors and individual sheaves were then pitched by men with pitch forks from the wagons and into an old threshing machine. The threshing machine was operated by an 80 foot endless grey-black belt about 18 inches wide, attached to the power wheel of a nearby idling tractor. The weathered silver threshing behemoth looked ancient even then, sitting on rusted cast iron wheels, spitting straw and chaff out the back, pouring grain from a big overhead spout, and spewing dust everywhere. This whole complicated process has been replaced by one machine—a combine, which cuts the grain (or picks it up from windrows), blows straw and chaff out the back while moving down the field, and pours the threshed grain into a truck driving beside the combine. Les and I tried this when I visited one long weekend in the fall, but we had to stop the combine to load the truck because I kept bumping into the combine while driving and looking out the back window of the truck lining up the spout. I was surprised Les was so casual about it. Normally, he was quite a strict guy.

I remember it being a "firecracker day," as they say in southern Alberta – about 98 degrees Fahrenheit in the shade. "Let's pack up the guns and do a little target practice," Les said as he came into the garage where Russ and I were "working" at the vice, trying to knock the gear off a rusted camshaft, or loudly hammering away at something equally productive. At thirteen and feeling the first urgings of manhood, I always enjoyed our forays across "the line." *Maybe I'd get close enough to look right into the eyes of a cute American girl, maybe even kiss her,* I would think to myself.

Although Les didn't say anything about crossing "the line" this time, Russ and I sensed his excitement. Crossing "the line" was always exciting – border guards in blue uniforms, donning shoulder flashes and epaulettes; the American guards carrying big side arms.

Russ L'Hirondelle, my second cousin (Grampa's sister's son on my mom's side) is a year or two older than me. At fifteen, and part Indian like me, he already had the dark shadow on his chin that I wanted. Just as we're closing the trunk on the two-tone orange and white '56 Mercury Crown Montclair with the guns in it, Russ's older brother Charlie drove into the yard in his shiny black '51 Ford coupe with all the windows rolled down. Although he was driving slow, the trunk looked like it was freshly dusted with fine unbleached flour.

"Wanna do a little target practice t'day?" asked Les.

"Sure, why not? dead-eye's my middle name!" Charlie's said, his red and white striped t-shirt pumping with laughter as it often did.

We roared out of the yard with the dual exhausts of the Mercury echoing off the barn. Poor Betty holding my little cousin Cindy in her arms probably couldn't even see us pass through the gate with all that dust temporarily suspended in the searing prairie sun. We bounced across the paved highway and headed west on a gravel road. *Humph, I thought we'd head down the highway to Coutts and Sweetgrass on the line.*

After making a number of turns, listening to *Tequila* on the radio with gravel pummelling the back wheel wells, and speeding way past Selby's place, we ended up on more of a trail than a road. With tall grass growing down the middle and tumble weed scratching the oil pan and Charlie sitting on the bench seat beside Les finally asked "where in the hell are we goin'?"

Les's pudgy right hand lifted off the thin white steering wheel and, with his palm temporarily facing the windshield while glancing over at Charlie, said "never you mind, you'll know when we get there."

We turned into a gully sprouting a few dusty poplars and light green tumble weed, wound our way down, and ended at a dump site. Russ and I immediately ran into the dump forgetting all about the guns. This was like a juvenile delinquents' heaven. We could break everything in sight with impunity. I picked up a big rock with both hands and heaved it through the front of an old TV set. I even thought I saw flames! Les, who repaired TVs, said the picture tube holds a charge even when it's not plugged-in and told me I probably *did* see flames and to be careful. Russ picked up an empty beer bottle, threw it, and when it popped against a large boulder, a million dark brown splinters were sprayed into the sun. This was too good to be true!

That's when I started wondering about all the beer bottles. There was much money here if we took them to the liquor store in Milk River. "Why didn't anyone else take them to the liquor store?" I asked Les.

"That's because they don't give a damn down here."

"We're in the States? We didn't go through customs?" I said.

"You forget I grew up here. I know this country better than any border patrol guard."

We loaded up the .22 and single shot 12 gauge shot gun, piled beer bottles in a pyramid, and stepped off about 50 feet. With the .22 we tried to shoot the bottom bottles in the pyramid and, before the ones higher up hit the ground, tried to hit them too. It took a little practice but we could do it with Les's semi-automatic and five shots loaded in the magazine. It was fantastic fun with broken beer bottles everywhere without worry about stray shots as they hit the sides of the gully. Les handed the loaded 12 gauge to Russ. When he fired at the beer bottle pyramid, I watched his forward foot jerk off the ground, with the recoiling, smoking barrel being wrenched to the sky. Russ said his shoulder hurt like hell, so I didn't fire the 12 gauge.

This was around the same time we also took the conventional route to the States, that way we could have supper in Shelby, Montana, go to a drive-in, and watch a movie that wasn't yet released in Canada. All I remember about a movie we saw one time was Russ and I sitting outside the car on the ground to stay cool, with the ground beside the car emanating a sweet cooling fragrance of thanks to be out of the blazing sun all day. But I do remember what happened just before the movie.

We were strolling along the main drag in Shelby, which wasn't much bigger than Milk River, when we heard the unmistakable snarl of a custom dual exhaust V8 Ford flat head coming toward us. As the car approached, I could see it was a red '52 Mercury Monterey Convertible with the top down, an eight foot whip aerial attached to the back bumper, with a thick fox tail tied at the top, blue sex lights in the windshield (that were supposed to cut down the glare of on-coming headlights at night, so they said), and two guys in white cowboy hats hoopin' and hollerin' with the radio blaring *Great Balls of Fire* as they sped by. I thought to myself: *look at those big shot Americans.* As they turned the corner, I just caught a glimpse of the License plate in the street lights: ALBERTA!

WHAT? These guys are Canadians? I don't know if anyone else in our group noticed, but I was silently embarrassed for these guys, and even more so for me.

A few years earlier on one of these vacations on the farm, Russ visited and we decided to collect bird's eggs by climbing the big poplar tree beside the one acre vegetable garden. I was in the lead, about 30 feet off the ground, and leaned out to grab a hand full of blue robin eggs when a branch snapped. Russ said I nearly knocked him out of the tree as I hurtled passed, but all I remember thinking was*: relax, you'll be okay.* When I hit the ground I heard my lungs and gasping voice trying to suck the air back in that was knocked out of me. I looked at the horizon of the flat prairie, my vision was filled with blood red hearts. I passed out. Instantly, I was at a dance hall with a Dixie land band playing. They were really good too and I especially enjoyed listening to the trombones as they ripped into their notes. Suddenly, I felt something shaking me but fought it off as I was listening to the music. It was my Aunt Betty. Later she said she was never so frightened in her life! There I was lying on the ground, apparently unconscious, but still able to fight.

They took me to the local doctor in Milk River. I can safely say he was useless – he said I was okay. Back home, Dr. Lobsinger said my right ankle was broken and I would have to wear a cast for three weeks. About six months later, my left knee was sore and had an odd swelling below the knee cap. When I visited Gramma and Grampa on the Rez, Gramma said I was moaning in my sleep. Although she wrapped my knee with a tensor bandage, she thought I had better go to the doctor. Dr. Lobsinger examined my knee and said it was broken, too, but only because it was left so long he may have to break it again before setting it correctly. Fortunately, he didn't have to. I wore the knee cast for six weeks and walked with a stiff leg for at least a month after the cast was removed. I remember laying on a gurney in the hall of the old Misericordia hospital after he removed my cast, looking down at my exceptionally skinny, hairy left leg which also showed evidence of being scratched with a long knitting needle. I was aching to bend my knee, which had been kept straight for six weeks.

I battled a voice inside saying *go on, bend it, no one is around, they'll never know. If you bend your knee it'll probably break again. Isn't that why it was in a cast in the first place, bonehead?* I was thankful when Dr. Lobsinger came into the hall. "Okay, egg collector, time for your new cast," he said.

Years later I read about a guy in a novel who broke his sternum. His description was exactly the way I felt for about two weeks after I fell out of the tree – every time I'd move, and especially when I'd push myself up and off the bed with my hands, there was a severe pain in my chest which left me gasping. In retrospect, I think this may have been a reckless adventure fraught with danger to gain love of my parents again. They immediately drove to Milk River after Betty cranked the handle on her party-line telephone to tell them what had happened.

Throughout elementary I remember becoming a sly bully, which was probably a family legacy. I wasn't the typical school yard jerk who tried to intimidate everyone, but I liked to pick on a few kids who were smaller than me, even some same sized kids who were still afraid of me. Bullying, though, I think, was my dad's, or even my granddad's, story in the beginning, too.

———

Granddad, Alexander Henderson Shennan, was born in Kirkcudbright, Scotland in 1886 and served in the King's Own Scottish Border Regiment in India and Egypt from 1902-1910. "Sandy," as he was generally known, came to Canada before 1914. Shortly after arriving, he served his new country with the Canadian Army during World War One. While overseas, he met and married Janet Drummond McLaren Burnett Sellar (Jennie), who was born in Glasgow, Scotland in1895. Sandy brought his new wife to the Westboro district of Ottawa where he joined his brothers in a blacksmith business. After a big disagreement, however, he and his wife moved west to Edmonton. My dad, William Shennan (a man with no middle name) was the second oldest. A few years later, the Shennans purchased a quarter section near Spruce Grove, Alberta and eventually raised a family of seven – Spruce Grove, named by the French and Scottish settlers in the 1890s (after groves of spruce trees in the area) evolved to a grain trading centre of around 400 people by the 1920s, complete with grain elevators, a hotel, a beer parlour, two churches, and a railroad located 20 miles west of the City of Edmonton (Alberta's capital city of 60,000 in the '20s on the northern edge of the prairie in the centre of the province). The Shennan's quarter section was on gently rolling deeded land four miles north of Spruce Grove and adjacent to the Michel Indian Reserve (which is how dad and mom met during the 1930s by attending a teen dance at Michael's school, located on the edge of the Rez near the Shennan's farm).

I never met dad's mom, Jennie. She died in 1944 when dad was overseas with the Canadian Army. Aunt Helen said my dad was always their mom's favourite – the little white rooster. Dad told me his father became angry often and one day literally threw him off a hay wagon while working in the field. My dad thought he broke his hip, which was never quite the same after that. It was one of many incidents before dad left home fed up at seventeen. He joined a threshing crew and said he worked all the way into Saskatchewan. Shortly after, he joined the Canadian Army, became a dispatch rider, and rode his motorcycle as far as Czechoslovakia during the Second World War.

One day in our new apartment on the second floor (when I finally had my own bedroom and a bathroom in our suite), I found a waxed cardboard box at the back of a deep shelf in the front hall way. It contained dad's war memories. Initially, I was excited to see the French cigarettes in their metal tin. When I lit one up and took a few drags, it burned so fast it crackled. Next was a pair of round, silver, metal-rimmed motorcycle sunglasses with leather patches beside the eyes to keep the glare out which almost fit, but then I discovered magazines. One was about the Canadian Army. Inside the first few pages were pictures of tanks and even dispatch riders on motorcycles, but toward the end, frightening pictures of men in gas masks. The second magazine had a picture of Hitler on the front and inside were pictures of executed Nazi generals and gruesome pictures of thousands of dead prisoners in mass graves at concentration camps, lying amongst the trees and stacked like cord wood on the ground. Underneath the magazines were German Maltese cross medals and Swastika shoulder flashes. I picked them up and, while I was holding them in my hand thinking about where they came from, started to shudder because I thought I could feel the presence of the dead German soldiers. *Did he kill these men?* I asked myself.

That was when I remembered asking my dad a few years earlier if he ever killed anyone in the war. "Don't ever ask your father that again!" my mom immediately spoke up.

The box ended up having a kind of macabre attraction for me. I would look in it often for years afterward when no one was home.

During my second time through grade three I put away the idea of quitting (I never factored failing, into the quitting scenario, I guess) so I passed with honours. Still, at home I was shaken to the core through experiencing one of the biggest realizations of my life – you don't really know another person, even when you live with them, trust them, and are close to you.

It was a grey cold March Sunday morning in 1954. I really didn't want to go out because I thought it was about minus 20 (the frost was higher on the windows than the days before when it was around minus 15). At 15 below, it wasn't too cold to skate, but at 20 below, my feet would get so cold that when I was walking home from the rink after skating, I would have to stop and sit down right in the middle of the icy sidewalk. My feet were too painful to walk on when they suddenly thawed out. We had moved to our three-room apartment by this time and that morning I was hanging around mom and dad's bedroom, lying on my side on their bed, propped up on one elbow. Both mom and dad said I should get some fresh air and go out and play for a while but I didn't want to go out in the cold. I just ignored their suggestions. Finally, dad walked over, grabbed my shirt just below the neck, pulled me off the bed with one hand, stood me up on the floor, and yelled from the back of his throat through his clenched teeth: "get out!"

I instantly felt like peeing, so I quickly put on my winter coat, boots, toque, and mitts and went to the bathroom down the hall. After I peed I sat on the floor. Dad knew I didn't leave the bathroom. When I heard the door of our suite slam and his socks thumping down the hall, I had no trouble peeing again as he banged on the bathroom door roaring: "you go outside!"

I went out the south door of the block leading to the top floor veranda and made my way down the three floors of outdoor stairs to the icy path below. I had no idea where to go or what to do. *What did I do wrong? Why was he so mad at me?*

I started walking toward the navy barracks kitty corner from Donald Ross School, and about half way along the diagonal path trampled in the snow across the school yard, I started to cry. I never felt so alone. Not knowing what to do, I went back to "The Block," stood on the top north veranda just outside the old bachelor suite where we used to live, and shivered for hours until the sun went down. When it was completely dark and I was so cold I couldn't take it anymore, I went back in. When I opened the door of our suite mom looked relieved.

"Dad is really sorry. We drove all over looking for you," she said. "We even walked in the crowd at the speed skating oval, but there were so many people we couldn't see if you were watching the races." I didn't say anything as I slowly took off my cold coat and boots, but I thought: *If dad was so sorry, why didn't he tell me himself?*

I learned, over time, that there are levels of trust through that incident. Although I knew my father and could trust him in most instances, like coming home and making our lunch at noon, or taking me goose hunting in the fall, I also learned I didn't know him as well as I thought. The notion made trusting him in every situation a little frightening. From then on, I approached dad with caution. I never knew exactly how he would react to me or my ideas – I was just like my dad in some ways.

Dad told me he promised himself when he became a father that he would never beat his kids like he was beaten when he was a child. Other than teasing me and holding me down for a whisker rub, he never physically abused me. I hated the whisker rubs mind you, since I felt so helpless being held down on the floor, yelling while he rubbed his rough beard on my cheeks, while mom shouted from the kitchen: "Oh, William, stop it! It sounds like he's dying." There was only one incident of physical abuse I remember in our family. That was when dad pushed mom down on the carpet when they were arguing. Both knees were bleeding and she went to see Dr. Lobsinger. When dad asked what the doctor said, mom told him: "a man like that should have his balls cut off." Dad stalled for a few days, but eventually went to see the doctor too. After that, he felt so remorseful he never used physical force against mom again.

But both Mom and I knew there were times you didn't dare to speak to dad, like the time he telephoned from work one day and said to me: "turn on the TV; a repairman is coming over this evening and I want it warmed up." I turned on the television and went out. The repairman came while I was out and left a note saying no one was home. When dad came home later that evening, he started shouting and swearing about all the long hours and hard work he does for his family, and couldn't I at least be there when he specifically asked me to stay home. I was too afraid to say anything and knew enough to keep quite when he acted like this, but he didn't ask me to stay home. He said the repairman was coming over "this evening" and all I had to do was turn the TV on.

Another time dad ordered a surfboard made of wooden strips that could be towed behind Uncle Bill's boat. We were excited and wanted Bill to pick us up, but when the surfboard was delivered that morning, it had a long crack down the centre strip. I was outside at the time, but mom said he went crazy mad cursing and pounding the board with the side of his fist. He specifically told the guy at the surfboard shop he didn't want the one with the long crack and even marked the one he wanted. After dad cooled down, Bill and Bessie came over. We exchanged the board on the way to Jackfish Lake. I think mom said something about overreacting, but she said it to him very cautiously that evening as we were coming home from the lake.

These instances aren't excuses or even reasons. Current literature on bullying, however, indicates that the home environment has much to do with the occurrences of bullying. The first incident I remember of deliberately bullying someone was when I was four or five years old. I cornered Kenny Smith, a cute little blond kid with black/brown eyes. I kept punching him until he cried. Kenny's mom was looking down from her second floor suite in "The Block" and yelled at me to leave him alone and stop beating him up. She must have told my mom too, because as soon as I came home, mom said: "if you keep beating up Kenny, his dad is going to catch you and pull your ears until they bleed." That did it. I didn't bother Kenny anymore; unless, of course, we were on the other side of "The Block" and I was sure his mom couldn't see me.

I was also on the receiving end of other kids' bullying, which may also be another possible explanation for my behaviour. About the same time I was beating up Kenny, Patrick Vandergaag would pick on me. One day he punched me in the mouth while we were skating on an outdoor rink our dads had just made in Renfrew's parking lot beside the block. I remember crying and feeling really sorry for myself when I rubbed my mouth and saw blood on my woollen mitt. I asked my dad what I should do about Patrick jumping on me from behind and dad taught me how to flip Patrick over my back. The next time Patrick jumped me, I quickly bent over like my dad taught me and, although Patrick didn't hit the icy rink as planned, he became more wary and stopped picking on me.

Another time at around seven years old, my dad's army buddy, Alf Pellant, who was also a Second World War dispatch rider, came to visit with his family. It was close to the time I was becoming ill with scarlet fever, and his son, Wayne and I, were playing with Dinky Toy cars when I punched him so hard in the stomach he howled. Everyone came running into the bedroom. I can still remember the smirk on my dad's face as if to say, "good for you, at least you aren't the one crying." My mom called the Pellants about two weeks later to see if Wayne was okay, not because I punched him, but because I was now quite ill and wanted to make sure Wayne wasn't getting sick too. She may have added that my illness was why I was so mean when they visited.

A couple of years later I was in the playground with Terry Chapman. We grew up across the hall from each other in "The Block." When my mom took us uptown, people would often comment about the cute little brothers, even though we weren't related. It was after school and Terry, who is quite athletic, was climbing on the roof of a little green house that the City of Edmonton Parks Department built to store summer equipment like paint brushes, paper, and soccer balls. Eugene Kliparchuk kept teasing Terry by pulling at his legs before he could swing them up on the roof. I could see it was dangerous since it was at least eight feet to the ground and Terry was losing his grip. I warned Eugene to leave him alone. Eugene kept chuckling while Terry was panicking and looking for a good place to land on the hard grass. I punched Eugene so hard in the mouth my knuckles split open. Terry scrambled up on the roof while Eugene held his face with both hands, blood streaming down from his nose and mouth and onto his shirt. When I got home, I told my mom what I did.

"Oh no! I wonder how big his mom is?," she said. Dad couldn't stop laughing at mom's reaction.

During my last year of elementary when I was 12 years-old in grade six, I recall my bullying coming to an abrupt end. It was a warm sunny day in June, just before summer holidays, and I was watching a mixed soft ball game being played by the grade nine students from McKay Avenue. I especially liked watching the grade nine girls with their recently developed breasts secretly bouncing behind their loose fitting sporty shirts, their buttocks rounding out their gym shorts, and their calf muscles flexing when they ran and pitched the ball. The girls liked me, too, teasing me about my black curly hair while I talked to them through the chain link fence. As I was standing there talking, I noticed out of the corner of my eye, Donny Dochuck and his little sister walking by.

Donny was about 20 feet away when I turned around and ran after him full tilt. He heard me at the last second, put his hand up to defend himself, but I tackled him. I quickly put him in a headlock and squeezed his head as hard as I could. When I was on top of him on the ground, he didn't put up much resistance, but managed to quickly take the hockey cards out of his shirt pocket and hand them to his little sister standing beside us. "Take these," he said to her in a quick panicky voice. The girls from MacKay started yelling at me: "Hey what the hell are you doing?"

I guess I was showing the girls how tough I was, but it seemed to have the opposite effect. *What the hell was I doing?* I thought.

While I was putting the pressure on Donny's head, time seemed to slow down. I could feel the warm sun penetrating my striped cotton T-shirt, right through to the skin on my back. I gazed down at the dirt smeared into the yellow stitching on the knees of my jeans that tore when I tackled Donny. I could hear a robin singing from the long line of poplar trees in the playground next to the ball field. I looked up at Donny's little sister standing about five feet away in her white cotton dress with the hockey cards pressed to her lips, and could see her eyes were terrified. She didn't know what to do to help her big brother. While listening to the dull slow thud of a softball being caught in a catcher's mitt, I gradually released the pressure on Donny's head, got off him, and we stood up and looked at each other while I dusted off my jeans. He was really apprehensive, breathing fast, and wondered what was going to happen next, but I just looked at him. "Sorry, Donny," I said.

His breathing slowed down a little when he turned toward his sister. They started walking away holding hands. I watched for a long time, while she gave the cards back to him, quickly looking over her shoulder, not believing I wasn't going to run after them again. I watched them until they went around the corner and disappeared at the end of the block.

I don't remember intentionally picking on anyone ever again after experiencing that moment of presence – that moment when time seemed to slow down and I could really feel and observe all that was happening. The calmness surrounding me only amplified my hurtful behaviour toward Donny and his little sister and showed me I wasn't impressing any girls by being a complete jerk. It was like an epiphany that day, which told me to start treating others the way I wanted to be treated and to not intentionally hurt anyone again.

Although bullying had become part of my past, not all of my friends followed suit. I remember skating really fast at the community rink one Friday evening in my early teens and coming to a stop at the boards. My feet were together and both blades sprayed the snow from the ice up the boards. A bit of it hit Pete Schurman who was already standing there. I had to bend over to tighten my skates. While in that position, Pete hit the middle of my back really hard with the side of his fist. I came up swinging. The first punch hit his stomach, the second his chest, and I was lining up to hit his lower jaw to knock him out, when he said "okay, okay! It was just a joke! you don't have to get so bloody mad!" It was a good thing we were on ice where it's difficult to really land a solid punch on skates. I may have hurt him. Pete seemed to respect me after that and didn't pull anymore "jokes." I guess I knew what it was like to be a bully. I just couldn't tolerate it anymore, even when it was directed at me.

Wesley Shennan

When I first went to McKay Avenue in Grade six, there was a soccer game – the guys from the flats against the guys from McKay. Many of the McKay students were orphans and lived at the Ex-Service Mens' Home for Children, just two blocks away on the top of the hill on 103 Street. Orphans learn at a very early age to defend themselves because they have to fight for everything, physically and verbally. While we were playing soccer, this big blond guy checked me when I didn't even have the ball. I made note of that and it happened again. So after it happened the third time, I intentionally tripped him and he fell face first on the grass and small roof stones that were left after repairing the roof at McKay. He picked up a hand full of stones. "I'm gonna wash your fuckin' face," he threatened.

*What in the hell am I going to do now? I can't run that's chicken, but I sure don't want those stones rubbed into my face until it bleeds (*as I learned later, his name was Roland Davidson). Just as I was figuring out what to do next, Richard Rutar, my buddy from the flats, stepped in and said: "Oh no you aren't."

They punched and wrestled on the ground for a long time until we broke them up once they were exhausted enough. The fight was a draw. That was the year there were too many of us from the flats attending McKay. I ended up back at Donald Ross to finish grade six. Richard, who we sometimes called Ricky, lived on the north side of 97th avenue. The School Board let him attend McKay. A few students living on the south side of 97th Avenue, like Susan Jamieson Petely-Jones, came to Donald Ross for their grade six (I mention her specifically because she was a pretty redhead who I had a mad crush on, but I never told her). Brian MacKenzie, my new buddy at McKay, told me Ricky and Roland would fight almost every recess and noon hour to see who the toughest was, but the teachers would come out to break them up. In the end, they never found out who was the best fighter.

———

There aren't many fights in the school yard today, partially due to teaching that bullying is not acceptable (which is a good thing). But many kids also carry weapons, like knives. Fights can now escalate to serious stabbings and, in some cases, death. There are campaigns that start in schools today, like "wear a pink shirt" campaigns, which assists in raising awareness against bullying gays. But in the workplace today, bullying still exists. It's been replaced by a new name: harassment, and remains a topic of on-going discussion and concern in the 21st century.

7. THE CAR CAREENED, ROLLED, AND BOUNCED 200 FEET

BEFORE I WAS OLD ENOUGH TO OWN A gun, I remember driving every fall to Beaverhill Lake east of Edmonton. Dad and I wore warm coats the same colour as the turning leaves, and as we crouched in the willows next to a big slough, I recall feeling an instant chill in the air as the sun poked us through the stubble. Dad nudged me with his elbow. When I looked at him, he was smiling. We maintained eye contact for a short while, and with slender smiles, we listened to the rails, coots, ducks, snow geese, Canada geese, and whistling swans. Whistling swans looked like snow geese from a distance, but didn't sound like geese when they flew over. It wasn't until we saw the huge black webbed feet dragging on the ground, as Uncle Ted bent its elongated neck over his shoulder and held its head with both hands next to his chest, that we instantly knew – an endangered species.

"Let's bury it, or drag it into the bush for the coyotes," Dad said. But Ted was determined. He took it home hidden the trunk of his *Austin*. He said it tasted good, too; like a goose.

I took my own young son goose hunting after work one day with my friend Gerry Shea and a guy I worked with, Dave Morgenstern. We drove east of Edmonton, toward Beaverhill Lake, and went to a farm about three miles from where dad and I used to hunt years earlier. Dave set his goose decoys. As a small flock of geese flew over, one dropped out and landed in the stubble.

"Draw a bead on 'im," we told Shea while yelling and clapping. As the goose took off, the piercing shot from Shea's double barrel twelve gauge jolted his head back, and the recoil instantly pointed the barrels skyward and jerking Shea's lead foot off the ground. The hot smell of gun powder, along with the first kill, fixed our veins with adrenalin.

A "V" of six Canada geese flew low over my son Waylon and me. I aimed just ahead of the leader and blasted three quick shots from my pump action twenty gauge. The leader was seriously hurt and flew lower and lower until he eventually tumbled and hit the open field. I broke into a ¼ mile sprint. He was laying in the stubble when I got there, but moved his head to get a better look at me. He held me motionless in his gaze for a 30 second hour, panting shorter and shorter breaths until his lungs burst with blood, and his life energy returned to the universe. I kept staring into those glazed eyes looking for the life that was just there, until my own eyes started to sting. When his mate flew in circles, around and around the stubble field calling and calling, I knew I couldn't kill animals anymore. I silently promised to never to hunt again.

It was years earlier in October when Dad and I drove past the Lindbrook Community hall on our way to Beaverhill. It was dark, but I could just make out black skid marks on the shoulder coming toward us; a broken guard post off to my right and tracks that went through the ditch and toward a gully. When I turned around and looked out the back window of our 1958 *Chevrolet*, I followed the flattened tall grass and, in the headlights of a car that passed the other way, had a brief glimpse of a leaning power pole and smashed-in pale yellow siding on the community hall. I didn't think much about it at the time as I looked out the back window. I had no idea how often those shattered boards would puncture my consciousness.

Wesley Shennan

My Métis buddies in Edmonton were Jim Branter and Gilbert Todd. We seemed to share this unspoken Métis bond. Gilbert's older brother, Bobby, was in his early 20s, married, and visited his parent's suite often as he lived in the same building (which was just down 101st Street from the apartment block I lived in). I remember Gilbert telling me he and his younger brother would sing a song when Bobby was around: "it takes a married man to sing a worried song." When Bobby heard the new words he started to laugh. "Okay, smart guys. Just wait until you're married and it's your turn."

Blain, Jim's older brother, was 19. One cold winter day after school, Jim and I went into the skating shed at Diamond Park to warm up. The two dimly lit rooms had a gas heater in the centre each, which looked like a burnt hot water tank standing on a piece of rusty boiler plate. Two inch black iron pipes surrounded the heaters and were bolted to the floor, and seemingly yelling, "stay away!" A continuous wooden bench was roughly nailed to the board walls and plank floor. Hockey players banged the back of their skate blades into the benches, so their heels would be forced snugly into their skates. There were splinters and slivers everywhere.

Jim started rolling on the floor in agony pretending he burnt his hand. The caretaker rushed into the room to see if everyone was alright. When he saw Jim, he smiled, shook his head, and went back into his little office. One guy started mouthing off: "you think you're pretty funny, eh? I think you look like the village idiot."

He walked over and started flicking a waxed yellow skate lace in Jim's face. He was older and bigger than Jim. It seemed quite unfair. When it looked like he wasn't going to stop, Jim ducked and ran outside.

Blain was watching a hockey practice when Jim told him about the bully. Blain came into the change room. "That's the son-of-a bitch over there," Jim said as he pointed. Blain grabbed the guy and slammed him hard against the wall. The guy wanted to fight, so Blain slammed him again and, with a quick powerful punch to the stomach, the guy slumped on the bench gasping for air. Jim's wide-open mouth was trying to smile. My eyes were probably as large as hockey pucks. *Wow, what a brother!*

The early snow floated like white goose down from a burst pillow when I was home alone reading the newspaper that October. It kept folding in my hands, but I wanted to read on. My eyes burned. I threw the paper on the floor, punched a cushion and threw myself on the couch.

"Why aren't you eating?" mom said. I kept thinking about what I read: four young Edmontonians were killed instantly and a fifth is in a Tofield hospital in serious condition. The high-powered Oldsmobile Rocket 88 careened off the highway, smashed a guard post, rolled down a small gully, struck a power pole 10 feet off the ground, and bounced to rest on what was left of its top – fenders, bumpers, the hood, the trunk lid and many instruments from the dashboard, including the clock, strewn in a 30 foot wide swath that led to the Lindbrook Community Hall. All occupants of the car were thrown from the vehicle and bodies of at least three of the four dead struck the front of the community hall with such force that the one-inch siding was shattered and splintered. One body hit the front wall with enough power to smash a gaping hole right through the one-inch siding and break the inner boards.

Milt Eaglesham was driving to Edmonton when he saw a wrecked car. He stopped to investigate. In the early morning light, he made the gruesome discovery of five crumpled bodies strewn between the overturned car and the community hall about 6:30 am. One body moved—it was Heather Sorensen, 18, and she was rushed to the Tofield hospital. Dead: Merle Smyth, 21, Hazel Kolskog, 17, James R. (Bobby) Todd, 22, and, Blain Branter, 19.

Were they screaming in terror when the car careened, rolled, and bounced for 200 feet? Were they unconscious when they went through the wall, or did they shriek in agony as their bodies crunched and broke through the rigid wood siding? Why did they die, when Gilbert and Jim and I live

Wesley Shennan

in our thirteen-year-old world of school, skating and girls? Will we die when we're 20? Did they die because they're part Indian like me? Why does God punish us? The thoughts would not leave me.

Dad and I kept hunting that October after the car crash. Every time we passed the community hall, the siding was slowly replaced and eventually painted.

Is that all there is to remember my friend's dead brothers? Newly painted shiplap? I would ask myself.

I didn't go to the funerals. I'd never been to a funeral and didn't know what to do or if I should even mention their names again to Jim or Gilbert. I remember Jim missing school after his brother died (Gilbert had just moved away before the car crash). That spring, Jim and I rode our bicycles to Gilbert's place on the south side, but Gilbert wasn't home. We visited with his mom hoping he would show up. While we were talking to his mom, I realized the woman with the two children, one a baby, was Bobby's wife. I didn't mention Bobby, but kept looking at her wondering how she was coping--a girl who just became a woman, now with two young children and no husband to love and support her.

I can't forget them. They were men I knew, not well, but well enough, and even if they contributed to my life in a small way, it's still there. Looking back, I think my first lesson in mortality was amplified by the warped idea that I belonged to a race that deserved suffering, persecution and death, if even by God himself. It made me treasure my fragile life, however long that would be.

8. GOD DAMN HALFBREED

I WAS TEN WHEN WE MOVED TO OUR SUITE
on the second floor. It had a bathroom in the suite and, for the first
time, I had my own bedroom. After school, I remember walking and
half running up the winding sidewalk flanked by a caragana hedge
to the Edmonton Public Library on top of MacDougall hill (near
the Hotel MacDonald), to take out books on decorating my room.
The books had great ideas, like moving the entrance a little way
into your bedroom room and putting your bed in the alcove created
beside the door (so when you entered the room you couldn't see
the bed); or, painting the walls the colours you wanted instead of
having your bedroom look like the rest of the house. Since we lived
in an apartment and my room was pretty small, I couldn't recess
the entrance (and I didn't think dad would let me paint the walls),
but that didn't prevent me from decorating it the way I wanted, like
stringing model airplanes (plastic ones I had built and painted) from
small hooks I screwed into the 12 foot ceiling; running a long aerial
wire from the crystal set beside my bed out a small hole I made in
the corner of the window frame and up the side of the block and
across part of the roof outside for better radio reception; building
a mini diorama for the plastic squirrel I assembled, complete with
spray-on fur; and putting up cut-out magazine pictures of singers
like Pat Boone, and later, a few "chicks" from *Playboy* magazine
(I don't remember mom or dad ever asking me to take them down).
My window looked south to the stairs on the second floor veranda

and beyond to the vegetable gardens, which were replaced by water treatment settling tanks of Edmonton's Water Treatment Plan when I was a teenager. In the summer, I kept my window open to listen to the robins early in the morning, and at night, to the diesel engines of distant semi-trailer trucks as they shifted and made their way up Walterdale hill on the south side. I had a book shelf, a clothes closet, and I studied on a fold-up card table – my own space!

The memories of the hot summer of 1957, when I spent a lot of time on the Rez with Gramma and Grampa, when I got up in the morning listening to Sam Cooke singing *You Send Me* on the radio downstairs, when Gramma was teaching me about goals and when we were smelling the deer in the bush; was the same time she told me we lived on an Indian Reserve and that I was part Indian, (which made me feel taller, browner. and confident). It was the most significant event in my ten-year-old life.

I recall thinking how everything fell into place: *that's why Grampa's brother, Uncle Fred, looked like a Chinaman, and why their adopted son, Joe, had such a good suntan all the time. That's why my second cousin, Wally Copick, when a little guy, told Gramma and Grampa to "stop speaking that Flench," when it wasn't French at all, but Cree.*

That summer, I started seeing and feeling "Indianess" everywhere.

I asked Grampa about the name Callihoo. He said it was an Iroquois word from Quebec that had something to do with a berry exploding in your mouth when you bit into it. I asked Gramma about tanning moose hide. I was surprised she knew how because we never did it. I assumed she learned when she was younger when she had to help her parents. She gave me a basic lesson: skin the animal, stretch the hide within a large round willow frame by punching holes on the outside edge of the hide and tying it to the frame with sinew, clean the skinned hide with a scrapper and remove all the hair, rub the brains of the moose with some other parts of the animal on the hide, smoke it close to a rotting spruce log fire (which doesn't spark and has lots of smoke) for two or three days, and, after smoking, take it off the rack, and chew and massage the hide between your fists to make it soft. There was probably more to it than that, but those were the basics I remember.

Gramma went on to tell me if wasps made their hives in the grass there would be little snow that winter, but if the hives were in the trees, the snow would be deep. She said she knew it was going to rain when the leaves on the trees in the front yard (the poplar clone) turned over and looked white (I learned, years later, that a change in atmospheric pressure, like low pressure associated with rain, flips the leaves over).

At about this same time, Gramma introduced me to organic farming, long before the term "organic farming" as understood today existed. She said she was concerned about the neighbours who were using fertilizer to make their crops grow and spray (herbicides) to kill all the weeds. She said the soil is full of bugs and worms, the creatures you can see, plus smaller life you can't see. All of these natural living things in the soil make things grow. With all the fertilizer and weed killer, she said, the soil is going to grow dependent. She was concerned, over the long term, that all of the natural things that make things grow were going to be replaced by chemicals, and that the only way crops could grow would be with fertilizer and weed spray. She said that Grampa would summer fallow the soil with a plough every second year to cut down on the weeds. The weeds that couldn't be reached with the plough next to the fence line would be pulled out by hand, both she and grampa walking around all of their fields pulling out the weeds like Canada thistle. Of course I didn't know it at the time, but her words were prophetic. Today, we consume genetically modified organisms (GMO), and companies like *Monsanto* have developed *Roundup*, GM seed, and bovine growth hormones – all infused with controversy, court cases, and investigations.

The same day Gramma told me we lived on an Indian Reserve and that I was part Indian, we drove the half mile east after supper to visit Aunt Bea, Wayne, and his little sister Joyce. I immediately asked Wayne: "did you know we are Indians and this is an Indian Reserve?"

Wayne was as surprised as I had been a couple of hours ago and looked at his mom. She nodded. Wayne and I looked at each other with broad smiles. Neither of us could believe it.

We started playing a game of hide and seek in the house and Wayne said: "Where's that tall Indian?" It felt great to be called an Indian. I know Wayne felt the same. I couldn't wait to get home and tell all my friends.

———

"You're a God damn Halfbreed," someone yelled while leaning over the railing on the second floor veranda of "The Block." The goose bumps started at the back of my neck, flushed along my jaw, and up my cheeks. I immediately picked up handfuls of loose roof gravel, which had been left on the ground after they repaired the flat roof on the block, and hurled one handful after another up at my so-called friends. "Okay, okay, Jesus Christ! Stop throwing those God damn stones!" I really didn't want to stop because I was so fucking mad, but I did. My friends went home. I lost friends over my proud announcement. I recall Peter Schurman shunning me for about six months. Our friendship, however, eventually returned, even though I never really felt quite the same about him.

Others would yell: "halfbreed" or "breed," riding by on their bicycles. They knew I was a walking volcano of anger whenever I heard these terms and they liked to taunt me. Very quickly, I learned not to share my identity with anyone, and because I don't have traditional features (I look more like a Greek or an Italian) I could slip by without really revealing who I was inside.

At first it was difficult. I was proud of being part Indian when I was ten years old, but at the same time knew I could only share this information with a select few: those I really trusted and those who had the same heritage as me, like Gilbert Todd and Jim Branter.

Wesley Shennan

After a while, it became a way of life to pretend to be someone from southern Europe. For example, I recall attending a Buffy St. Marie concert at the Jubilee Auditorium in Edmonton when I was 18, when I overheard one of my friends say "not bad for a hop-jiggy." I felt my volcano erupting and wanted to punch someone, even the wall, but said to myself: *okay, okay, okay, okay* until my anger subsided and no one was aware how crazy I was inside.

A few years earlier, when I was ten and told Gramma about the reaction of my friends, she looked at me for a long while with a profound sadness in her eyes.

"Well it's a good thing you look the way you do, because it isn't obvious at first glance you're part Indian. It's not a good idea to tell anyone that you have Indian blood in you," she explained. I didn't think a lot about what she said at the time or why both she and Grampa, or especially my mom, were so anxious to cover up who they were. They would not talk much about their history, their culture, the Sundances they attended, or the fact they lived on an Indian Reserve. In retrospect, I can see why this time in my life was very difficult for me.

A few years before learning about my Indian heritage, mom started working. I felt abandoned. I became a rebellious delinquent and decided to quit school (but unexpectedly failed grade three instead). I felt like a total loser and withdrew into myself. Then dad threw me out of the house in the winter and I felt I couldn't trust my own father. Now, at ten years old, I learned I was part Indian and initially felt so proud, confident, and brown, but suffered whenever I told anyone. To top it off, both Gramma and mom said it was a good thing I looked the way I did, since they themselves were really ashamed of being Indians. Without saying as much, they taught me to be the same.

I became proud of my heritage and ashamed simultaneously. I remember sitting alone in my room at the fold-up card table, where I planned to do my homework after school before mom and dad came home. But I got up from the table and went out my bedroom door. The sun was shining through the grey and red floral drapes mom made to cover the three tall windows in the front room as I walked across the yellow patterned carpet which was laid over the creaky maple hardwood floor. I went past the cupboard in the front entrance with the grey and red stripped curtain to hide the deep plywood selves and past the beige entrance door with a plywood insert in the door where a glass window used to be, and an inset piece of plywood in the transom window overhead. I went into the kitchen with the newly laid yellow and brown stripped tile on the floor and entered the walk-in pantry which had a green and white gingham checked curtain for a door. The pantry was well stocked with stacked yellow, green and red cans of store-bought fruit and fish, homemade canned pickles in clear glass canning jars (with the dill floating like weeds in rows of cylindrical green aquariums), cast aluminium pots and pans with small nicks and pits, and black bake-o-lite handles. Grapefruit, bread, and butcher knives were neatly laid out on a lower shelf which was covered in a pale yellow checkered oil cloth. I picked up the sharp 12 inch butcher knife with its faded brown wooden handle with three silver rivets, held it firmly with both hands, and poked the blade up into my stomach until it hurt and almost broke the skin through my shirt.

I can still remember saying to myself out loud: "if you ever fail again, you push this knife up into your stomach until it hits your heart!" I stood there for about 30 seconds wondering what it would feel like, and then put the knife back on the shelf, and went back to my room.

Thankfully, I didn't fail another grade, but looking back, it was more than just failing that was troubling me. Everything fell in, from mom's working to dad's bullying. But I think one of the most profound revelations at that time was learning to be ashamed of being part Indian. I was taught to lie about who I am, avoid all discussions about my heritage, and cover-up all "Indianness."

Where does the shame of being an Indian, a Métis, an Inuit, a Native, a First Nations person, an Indigenous person, an Aboriginal, an Amerindian come from? (I purposely didn't include the word Halfbreed. The Métis Nation today embraces the term, and says it's only the English equivalent of the French word Métis. To me it sounds like you aren't a thoroughbred and that you'll never amount to anything more than half of anyone else. Métis, on the other hand, embraces the best of both worlds, to me at least, and doesn't make you feel inadequate.) Why should anyone be ashamed of who they are? It certainly isn't something inherent in their own culture, is it? In my family, as in most, it seems being ashamed can be traced back to the colonial teachings learned in residential school, passed on and down through families, and then reinforced through general racism in mainstream Canadian society.

However, there has been more than just the impact of residential school over the past 400 years. Canadian Indigenous communities have been subject to wave after wave of debilitating shocks and traumas since the first large-scale European contact in the 1600s. These shock waves have come in many forms, as listed below (paraphrased primarily from *Mapping the Healing Journey*, 2002):

- Diseases. Diseases such as influenza and small pox (often introduced on purpose by distributing infected blankets), measles, polio, diphtheria, tuberculosis, then at a later time, diabetes, heart disease and cancer;

- Destruction of traditional values and economies with colonization and expropriation of traditional lands and resources;

- Undermining traditional identity, spirituality, language, culture and family units through missionization, residential schools and government day schools;

- Destruction of traditional forms of government, community organization and community cohesion through the imposition of European governmental forms as imposed by the *Indian Act*, the Indian Agent and the elected chief and council system, which systematically sidelined and disempowered leadership and governance as well as fracturing traditional systems for maintaining community cohesion and solidarity;

- Finally, the breakdown of healthy living patterns in individuals, families and community life, plus the gradual introduction of alcohol, many different drugs, their associated abuses, family violence, physical and sexual abuse, loss of ability to maintain relationships, loss of ability to care for children, depression, anger, rage and increased levels of interpersonal violence and suicide.

What this has meant is that as many as three to five generations removed from externally induced trauma, the great great grandchildren of those originally traumatized, are now being traumatized by patterns that continue to be recycled in families and communities today. This partially explains the passed-down colonial teachings from residential school that came to me through my Gramma and Grampa and my mom – to be ashamed of being Indian!

By 1900, there were 64 residential schools staffed by missionary teachers throughout Canada (many of whom had no grasp of pedagogy), and who gave vocational, manual, and especially religious, instruction. Although initiated in the 1600s in New France, it wasn't until the 1830s when mainly the Roman Catholic and Anglican denominations, in cooperation with the colonial governments and later the Canadian federal government, began to formally establish residential schools for Indigenous peoples throughout the Country. Residential schools were viewed by colonial, and subsequently by the Canadian federal authorities, as the ideal system for educating Native people because they removed children from the influences of traditional family and tribal life. Traditional education amongst North American Aboriginals was accomplished by observation, practice, family and group socialization, oral teachings, aural learning (especially in music), and participation in tribal ceremonies and institutions. These methods did not remotely resemble the dominant tradition of classroom education practiced by the Europeans, the primary component of the residential school (mainly from *Shingwauk's Vision*, 1996).

An interesting insight to traditional family and tribal life was recently explained to me by a member of an interior British Columbia Indian Band, Penticton. She told me the child was always viewed as the centre of tribal life – a child-centred society. Viewed in a series of circles, with the child at the centre, those immediately surrounding the child were the elders responsible for teaching the child history, customs, mythology, meaning and life purpose. Beyond the elders, in another surrounding circle, were the mothers and fathers responsible for food, clothing, shelter, protection, and day-to-day survival skills. When the residential school system was instituted in the 1830s, it not only took the children away, but it also removed the whole purpose for, and focus of, tribal life (it is interesting to compare this model to current Canadian society, with elders shuffled off to senior's homes, kids shuffled off to school, and moms and dads being the centre of society, trying to provide everything for old and young). It is no wonder most native people viewed the residential school system as harsh and cruel. Not only were the children taken away with tribal life was left in shambles, but the children, having once arrived at school, were physically punished for disobedience, forbidden to use their native languages, and made to feel ashamed of their native identity. Many children also suffered sexual abuse in residential school. But it was the policy, as well as the legislation through the *Indian Act*, of forced enculturation and assimilation being directed at all of Canada's First Nations and Native People in general, that had the broadest impact.

One of thousands of examples of the effect of residential school is provided by Sarah Jerome, the Language Commissioner of the Northwest Territories in 2010 and residential school survivor. To paraphrase what she said: ...before I entered residential school, I was 100% healthy physically, mentally, spiritually and psychologically. But after the foreign food, new clothing, rules, prayers, church everyday, told when to sleep and nap, I couldn't make up my own mind, I had no opinion. If I said: "I don't like this food," I was punished. When I graduated 12 years later I felt like a robot, confused and living between two worlds. Doreen Reid, sharing at the same event in Yellowknife in October, 2010, said "there were times when I tried to scrub my skin, scrubbing off the brown, because I wanted to be white."

My Gramma and Grampa met each other and attended Dunbow Residential School (St. Joseph's Industrial School and also called the High River Industrial School) in the early 1900s. Located on the banks of the Highwood River near the Town of High River, Alberta, south of Calgary, Dunbow opened in 1888 and closed in 1924. The school was over two hundred miles south of the Michel Indian Reserve. It was probably around 1960, when I was 13, that I remember driving with my parents, as well as Grampa and Gramma, to visit my aunt Betty on her farm near Milk River in Southern Alberta. We were on the highway south of Calgary and passed near the location of Dunbow Residential School, when Grampa said: "I always feel happy here because this is where I went to school." Gramma looked at him a bit surprised. "Well, I'm glad you feel happy about going to school there," she said.

Other than Grampa telling me he remembers a pretty young girl waving to him from the girl's residence, (Gramma), this is my only recollection of any discussion I heard regarding my grandparent's attendance at residential school. Today, I do have two original post cards Grampa sent to his mom Nancy Callihoo on the Michel Reserve both dated 1912. In both cards, Grampa is working with his classmates in the field and the tone of the cards seems upbeat. One reads: *"Dear Mother, I am going to write a few lines could you know me in this picture I sit on the disk* (he was in the picture on the postcard showing a huge steam-driven tractor towing a double disk and harrows on the wide flat prairie). *I guess that's all to say in this post card. From Solomon Callihoo."*

Wesley Shennan

Life may have been a bit easier for Grampa. Although he had classic First Nation features, high cheek bones, a strong prominent nose and full lips, he also had blue eyes and blondish hair. His nick name on the Rez was "Dutchy." Gramma, on the other hand, (the pretty girl waving from the girl's residence), had similar cheek bones, a prominent nose, and full lips, but with black wavy hair and brown skin. There was no mistaking her First Nation heritage.

What they both absorbed, however, through their residential school experience was a deep feeling of being ashamed (mom was home schooled and didn't attend residential school, but acquired the same ashamed feeling and teaching from Gramma). Why? Why were they all ashamed of being Indian and why did they pass this on to me? After reading a number of books, periodicals, and news stories about residential school, including that of Doreen Reid who wanted to wash the brown off her hands so she could be white, it is very evident that being made to feel ashamed was prevalent. But this still doesn't explain why. Why were First Nations in Canada made to feel this way?

In his autobiography, Mahatma Gandhi describes the imposition of a colonial attitude to make one feel ashamed, and Rina Kashyap, writing a paper in 2005, explores it further. Here is some of what she says:

> The premise of this paper is that the colonizer institutionalizes humiliation as a strategy to control the colonized......an inevitable consequence of the power dynamic......between the colonial master and the colonial subject..... culture and system of humiliation lends support to colonialism.....Gandhi's philosophy of non-violence......(is) a strategy to subvert this system of shame and humiliation...
>
> Humiliation is a strategy to mask the unjust and exploitative nature of an oppressive activity. It

seeks to dis-empower and disable its victim. It assumes many forms; verbal and nonverbal. The practice manifests in social, cultural, economic, and political contexts. It is **most powerful in the realm of ideas** (my emphasis) where it 'discourses' itself as legitimate. This legitimacy makes humiliation appear as a just dessert, thereby making opposition to it illegitimate.

The argument of the 'civilizing mission' was colonialism's attempt to seek legitimacy for an enterprise that was essentially exploitative. The... colonizer justified it almost as a humanitarian act. It was argued that the native had to be freed from the 'heathen' practices and customs. ....Colonies were looked upon and understood as backward and primitive, in need of guidance to the path of modernity (a further exposition of colonialism used for this paper is contained in the references).

Of course, hand in glove with this system of shame and humiliation is colour prejudice. To paraphrase Gandhi, he says the hardship to which I was subjected was superficial; only a symptom of the deep disease of colour prejudice.

So now the picture is more complete. Not only is humiliation a colonial mask to justify exploitation, but it, along with colour prejudice, makes the victim completely shamed and disabled – there is no way out and there hasn't been a way out for many First Nations for too long.

Regarding prejudice and racism in Canadian Society, J.R. Miller in *Shingwauk's Vision,* writing in 1996, states:

Assumptions of racial superiority by Euro-Canadians were not unique to Native/non-Native relations. In fact, by the late nineteenth century white-skinned Canadians were very much inclined to look down on people of different hues for several reasons. New strains of scientific racism such as Social Darwinism, the influence of British Imperialist attitudes, and the spill over from the institutionalized racism that survived the Civil War and emancipation in the neighbouring United States combined to influence Euro-Canadian society strongly in a racist manner... Canadians who identified with the Caucasian race usually held condescending attitudes towards non-white peoples.

Similarly, racist assumptions now applied specifically to Indians, underlay policy towards Natives in the decades after the making of the treaties. Indian Affairs officials and missionaries recognized that Aboriginal peoples often held to different values, even if those values were usually decried rather than celebrated. And both officials and missionaries generally recognized that Native peoples organized their lives differently from Euro-Canadians. The problem was that bureaucrats and educators tended to assess Indian ways against the standard of their own society: Indian culture was defective because it was different. The deputy minister of Indian Affairs expressed this view early in the century when commenting on the difficulty that Ottawa and the churches were experiencing in changing Indians' behaviour. 'It must not be forgotten,' wrote Frank Pedley, 'that we are working in a material that is stubborn in itself; that the Indian constitutionally dislikes work and does not feel the need of laying up stores or amassing wealth. The idea which is ingrained in our civilization appears to be that a race must be thrifty and must surround itself with all manner of wealth and comforts before it is entitled to be considered civilized. The Indian had not yet reached that stage, and it is doubtful if he will...' (reprinted with permission of the publisher).

To summarize, I now understand more fully the history, the reasons, and the depth of feeling ashamed to be an Indian. It is more of a trauma than a teaching. A trauma is an emotional shock, sometimes following a stressful event, leading to long-term neurosis. The emotional shock for me was initially feeling so proud of being part Indian when I was ten years old, but not only having my proud feelings scorned by racist attitudes in society, but also being told by my Gramma and mom to hide it and to lie. It is like a neurosis to pretend to be someone you aren't. You always feel like you'll be uncovered and discovered.

I can see now why I was told to be ashamed. It is a totally unacceptable institutionalized humiliation, central to the colonization not only taught in residential school, but reinforced throughout society by the equally unacceptable belief of racial superiority. These attitudes have been passed on to us for three to five generations. We subconsciously believe this stuff is true! It isn't. And I will not be ashamed to be part Indian for as long as I live! I am celebrating my proud 20,000 year heritage in this country! However, arriving at this point in my life hasn't been without its struggles.

9. A WHITE MASK

I NEVER WENT BACK INTO THE PANTRY to hold the butcher knife to my stomach again. In retrospect, I think one of the main reasons was getting a pet budgie bird "Bud." Bud came into my life shortly after we moved to our apartment on the second floor. I bought a book about raising young parakeets, and soon after, he was saying "pretty bird, shut up you shit" and flying around the house looking for his morning toast. Dad cut the corner off his toast and Bud would instantly land on his hand to nibble a trough down the centre, leaving crumbs all over the table like he was splitting the seeds in his cage. When it was bath time, he didn't hesitate to dip over again repeatedly into the little yellow plastic bathtub with a mirror on the bottom, shake and shiver his wings and continue to make it rain all over the kitchen sink, the counter and the floor. He had moods too. When he was angry, he would purposely fly closer to your head than normal, making sure his wings made an unusual noise while wiggling his tail then landing on an unfamiliar perch, like the rod holding the green checked gingham curtain covering the pantry entrance.

When I was teaching him a new word, I would sometimes tease him by moving my lips, not saying anything, and he would instantly bite my lip as if to say "speak up." When I got older and rolled into the yard in my '59 Chevy with the noisy pipes, he would start chirping loudly, even if it was four in the morning. I'd have to come upstairs and say hello to him through the cover over his cage to calm him down. It seemed like he thought logically. He didn't just repeat the things I taught him, but learned words on his own and used them at the appropriate times like saying "take'im out" when I walked by his cage in the morning. Looking back, I think Bud helped me by taking the focus off of me.

In many ways, he saved my life.

When I left home at nineteen to be a tour guide at the Columbia Icefields, I told all of my new friends and acquaintances, including Bill Ruddy, my employer at Snowmobile Tours Limited, that I was Scottish Canadian (which was half of the truth) and conveniently left out the fact that I was also part Indian. I felt pretty confident about my looks because, just a year earlier, I learned in high school Social Studies that southern Scots often had darker skin and black curly hair because Great Britain was occupied by the Romans and they intermarried. The perfect alibi: here I was, a Roman-looking Scot because of intermarriage. I just conveniently left out the details of what intermarriage.

Covering up my Indian heritage wasn't only a conscious effort. I can see in retrospect that it became more of an ingrained, unconscious belief, since I really began living an internal life of shame and humiliation. I didn't feel proud of my Indian heritage like I did when I was ten years old and I gradually began feeling it was more of a nuisance. After a while, I didn't even become upset at racist slurs about Indians – I just ignored them – I began wearing a white mask. I fell right into the colonial institutionalized shame and humiliation. Pretending to be white allowed me to escape colour prejudice, the "enforcer" of shame. No matter where I went to school, where I worked or played, such as the ski hill, I escaped the enforcer. But inside there was turmoil. I wasn't being true to my roots, my mom, my ancestors, and all this constant covering up and avoidance made me feel cautious and timid. I lacked confidence in situations where I might be revealed, like feeling compassion for Indians when the racist slurs began. I learned, and internalized, that I had to be quiet even when I really didn't want to be.

I lived in internal shame, humiliation, and denial until approximately my mid 30s, when I actually surprised myself one day by blurting out in public that I was part North American Indian (a little more on this later). Basically, from the time I left home at 19 until my mid-thirties, I wore a white mask to conceal my true heritage.

Honya, the curvaceous petite blond with the deep blue eyes I met at the Columbia Icefields, married me January 8, 1968, when I was 21 and she was 22. That summer we were the surprised parents of a nine pound, four ounce baby boy, Waylon. Two months before he was born, Honya and I were listening to records with Brian MacKenzie and his grandfather Percy Hansen. Percy was a retired Executive Director of a number of Young Men's Christian Associations (YMCA's) across Canada and was now making way more money as an artist than he ever did with the 'Y' – after retirement he studied with someone closely associated with the Group of Seven (a group of Canadian landscape painters active from 1920 to 1933).

"Who wrote that last song?" I asked Percy. Brian grabbed the cardboard album cover, flipped it over and read the credits, "It says Waylon Jennings." None of us had ever heard of this guy, but when Honya and I heard that name, we looked at each other and instantly knew that if we had a boy, his name would be Waylon.

I remember the day of his birth very clearly. I had managed to obtain a job as a Chemical Plant Operator at Dow Chemical in Fort Saskatchewan, about 30 miles northeast of Edmonton. I absolutely hated the smell of the place and the shift work (especially the seven days of grave yard shift from midnight until eight in the morning), running distillation towers and making ethylene glycol, or antifreeze; but it wasn't as bad a job as the guys next door who took their street clothes off in one locker room, walked through a shower, and put on their work clothes in another locker room, because they made 2,4,5-T, a deadly herbicide. They used to joke that it was the only place in the world you had to wash your hands before you took a piss because the herbicide residue really burned your skin.

The pay was excellent though for a guy with limited experience and fresh out of high school. I started out at six hundred bucks a month, and within six months, I was making almost seven hundred a month in 1968 (most guys working for the City of Edmonton at the time were making around $2.75 per hour, which was roughly $440 per month).

It was an early sunny August morning and I was getting ready to go to Dow for the day shift when I heard Honya's frantic words from the kitchen in our little apartment on 118th avenue and 53rd street in Edmonton: "Wes, my water broke!"

I bolted from the bedroom and saw her silhouette in the kitchen window – a stooped bulging nighty hanging onto the counter, legs apart, and her eyes focussed on the water running down her legs.

"Do you feel pain, are you having contractions?" I asked.

"No," she whispered, still hanging on to the counter.

"I'll call the plant."

After just two rings John Vandermeer answered. "Sorry man, any other day I would cover for you, but I have a final exam this morning," he said.

I knew John wasn't giving me a line; it was the second week in August, the week of final exams for university summer school. John, like many of us, traded his day shifts so he could go to school in the day and still work afternoons and grave yards.

"Can't you even take me to the hospital?" Honya demanded, still hanging onto the counter.

"No, I can't," I said reluctantly, "John has a final exam this morning, but I'll call a cab and ask the guy who comes in at four to come in early so I can be with you. I'll come to the hospital as soon as I can."

"You don't have to call a cab right away. Sometimes water breaks early," she said, pushing herself away from the counter and standing up straight. "I feel good. I'm not having contractions and I'm only gonna go in when they start."

I was really surprised at what Honya had just said. After the initial shock and excitement of it all, she seemed to be relaxing, and probably, I was now more excited than she. "Okay, I'll phone you as soon as I get to the plant, and if you don't answer, I'll know you've gone in."

The old black bustle-back 1961 Volvo took me to work in a daze that day. At 10:30 Leo Casper came in to relieve me a full hour and a half before he had to. "Go on get outta here! You can't leave her all on her own."

I always liked Leo. We didn't work the same shifts, but sometimes he'd come in early and we'd discuss the "duster novels" we both read.

"You know, I once believed all that manly bullshit, like be tough, never back down in a fight and don't be afraid to defend your honour," I remember Leo saying once, "but even when I won a fight, I knew I still lost. Imagine, I actually tried to live that phony, cowboy philosophy at one time."

Leo had just expressed in a few words what I felt, but I didn't know exactly what I felt or how to express my feelings about being a "real" man, as described in these novels. All I knew for sure was I didn't really believe it. I didn't want to go around fighting everyone at the slightest provocation or affront to my honour. Leo summed it up nicely. He actually tried to live like the duster novels said we should. He failed, knew why, and expressed himself very succinctly.

Before Leo arrived, I telephoned home and there was no answer. It was close to noon when I arrived at the old Misericordia Hospital on 110th street, just a block west of the high level bridge. By now Honya had been in labour for five hours.

"How ya doin'?" I asked.

"I've started contractions; I'm okay until they start, but then it's very uncomfortable."

By the look on her face I knew it was way more than "very uncomfortable." It probably hurt like hell, but she was trying to put on a brave front. The nurse with the German accent said I should massage her lower back. As I did, Honya rolled from her side, got up on her knees, and held onto the side bed railing.

"Don't let her get up," the nurse said in a loud German voice as she came back into the room, "she could fall out, and how would you feel zen?"

Years later, Honya and I learned that kneeling was a very common means of giving birth for Indigenous peoples all over the world, but, of course, not practiced by the "superior" knowledge of Western medicine. For some reason, lying on your back (maybe to make it easier for the surgeon?) became the standard means of giving birth.

Honya's gynaecologist, Dr. Genser, broke his leg sky diving, so he was replaced by Dr. Schultze. Schultze, blond about 5'11" and 15 years older than me, had a look of intelligent confidence. I felt at ease when he explained "I can see the baby's head and I'll have to use forceps; it's sometimes necessary with big babies and small girls."

"Can I be there when the baby is born?" I asked.

Before Schultze could answer, the nurse blurted "of course not! Ve can't have zat. You stay outside in za vaiting room."

At 8:58 pm, August the 12th, 1968, music began playing over the public address system, accompanied by crying from the delivery room. The nurse opened the doors a crack and said "it's a boy" to me, but before I could even get up off the chair, she closed the doors again. About five minutes later she came out of the room holding a white bundle close to her and began rushing down the hall. "Hey!" I shouted as I quickly got out of my chair, "is that my son?"

She stopped and said "Oh yes, yes, you have a quick look, ve have to clean him up."

Well, he did need cleaning. I couldn't tell if all that dark brown hair and red complexion was his own or because of all the blood. About half an hour later, a gentle smiling nurse held a crying nine pound, four ounce bundle to the window in the nursery. He looked perfect (I learned somewhere that Down's Syndrome newborns have fingers all the same length, which wasn't the case here) and he had two legs and lots of dark brown hair – *a little Indian-looking*, I thought. While I was looking him over and the nurse patiently held him to the window, he stopped crying. I also read that newborns cannot focus, but he seemed to be the exception, as he looked straight into my eyes, searching my soul as if to say: "So, who are you? Why are you looking at *me*? Why are *you* here?"

So, I said to my son: "Hi Waylon."

I stayed at Dow for four and a half years, attending the University of Alberta during the day, and working afternoons and graveyards. When the distillation plant was running smoothly there was lots of time to study, as all we had to do was watch the pressures and temperatures, take samples and analyze them at the beginning of the shift, and read tank levels at the beginning and at the end of every shift. Guys were studying to be Stationary Engineers and going to University like me. We became popular, having traded all of our day shifts for the unpopular afternoons and graveyards. Meanwhile, the poor buggers next door were making their powerful and overwhelmingly pungent herbicide in batches, running all shift opening and closing valves, controlling chemical reactions, with little time, if any, to study.

Working hard *to make a better life for my family*, I thought, became a pattern. After graduating with a Bachelor of Science degree in Physical Geography, with a host of minor arts courses about Indigenous Peoples, I ended up in community planning. I still didn't know what I really wanted to do, so I bought a little 700 square foot house that felt like a cottage in the Highlands Community of Edmonton (not too far from our little apartment on 118th avenue and 53rd street) and joined forces with my father-in-law John Androsoff, who was a journeyman carpenter.

John, Honya, and I made the little cottage into a 900 square foot home in under a year. I did all of this during evenings and weekends while working full-time as a planner with the Edmonton Regional Planning Commission. After finishing the upstairs part of the house, John went back home to B.C., but I continued the building by gutting the basement and refinishing it in the same style as the upstairs, which included a sound proof room so we could play loud music on guitar and drums (Waylon had become quite an accomplished drummer / percussionist and played classical music for a year with the Edmonton Youth Orchestra by this time).

As soon as the basement was finished, I didn't stop. During my mid 30's, I decided to return to university for a year (in Scotland) and work toward a Master of Philosophy degree in Urban Design and Regional Planning. My planning career needed to grow, *to make a better life for them.* I kept pushing myself with this thought.

Scotland was a little reprieve from the pattern of work, work, work. I followed Pierre Trudeau's study suggestions mentioned in one of his books: eight hours study, eight hours rest, and eight hours for yourself. It worked. I had more relaxed time with Honya and Waylon. This is when I felt more reflective and thoughtful about whom I really was. I surprised myself when I was riding in a car with my student colleague Juan de la Pena, from Mexico along with his wife-to-be Nicky and his future mother-in-law, talking about family roots and how important they were to our being.

"Yes," I can remember saying. "That's why I'm here, my dad's family is from Scotland." I probably planned to leave it there and not mention my mom as I had learned to do throughout the years, but Juan's future mother-in-law asked "what's your mother's background?"

I can remember suddenly feeling almost the same as I did when I was ten as I blurted "North American Indian," with great pride. I also felt inwardly shocked, thinking *did I really just say that?*

This was the beginning of my journey, albeit a very small step away from institutionalized humiliation and shame. My personal reflections in Scotland were probably aided by a broader societal recognition of Native North Americans, as depicted in the movie

Little Big Man, starring a real Indian, Chief Dan George from the Tsleil-Waututh Nation across the inlet from Vancouver, B.C, as well as in books like *The Unjust Society*, written by Harold Cardinal, a Cree from Alberta. These works and their acknowledgements helped me release the burden of colonial suppression.

As soon as I came back home, the relentless pattern of work, work, work (*make a better life for them*) returned. I wrote my Master's thesis during evenings and weekends of the second year of the two-year program (in my new office/guest bedroom in the basement) while working full-time with the planning commission. I began to ignore my family again and ignore my inner reflections of who I really was.

Needless to say, ignoring my family in order to make a better life for them than I had, created a void. I remember Honya begging me to just once watch the eleven o'clock news with her as I wrote my thesis in the adjacent room.

"Just a few more sentences," I can remember saying. Of course, the few more sentences were never done until she and Waylon were usually in bed fast asleep. I was proving myself as a successful, hardworking white guy at the expense of my small loving family.

Honya and I mutually agreed to separate in July, 1985, just one year after I graduated from university the second time. She moved to Victoria and Waylon stayed with me to finish high school. Waylon and I became skiing buddies for a couple of winters. I read in a self-help book about separation and divorce that instructed you shouldn't rely on your children for emotional support. I didn't share anything with him about my feelings. I was hard on myself to be an accomplished white man in society and took this hardline, high standards approach with everything and everyone, without really ever questioning, *What did I really want from life? Who am I really? What did I need in a relationship with my son? What are his needs?* I remember feeling extremely sad and alone after Honya left and decided I did not want to be by myself for the rest of my life.

I eventually re-married in 1988. At the wedding ceremony, I remember telling the master of ceremonies to make sure he told the crowd of 120 that I was part Indian. *Wow*, I thought *I did it in front of all these people, half of whom I don't even know.* I looked for the guests' reactions, but there weren't any I could perceive, except my cousins who looked as proud as I felt.

A bill was passed to amend the *Indian Act* in 1985, Bill C-31, which said that women like my mom who married non-Indians like my dad were no longer considered non-Indians and could apply to have their Indian Status re-instated. This bill also allowed the children of these marriages to apply for Indian Status. With that, I received my Indian Status Card in 1988, which was one of the reasons I made this proud announcement at my wedding. Because the legislation has been amended again in 2011 to allow grandchildren to receive status, Waylon also has Indian Status Card.

Shaking off the shackles of institutionalized shame and humiliation wasn't easy, though. In 1992, at my dream job interview to be the Executive Director of the South Peace Regional Planning Commission in Grande Prairie, Alberta, I remember being asked if I spoke Cree. I thought *I can't tell them about my background. I might not get the job*, I answered the question with a curt "no." I did get the job, but always felt I wasn't being true to myself or my ancestors by not elaborating, saying "I don't speak Cree, but I do hold an Indian Status Card." Looking back, it's really amazing how strong and engrained this shame and humiliation is about being an Indian.

10. BEYOND THE RESTRICTIONS OF A DOCTRINAL BOX

MEETING THAT LITTLE BROWN MAN IN the hallway when I was four-years-old introduced me to the spirit world. Ever since that encounter, I've believed in spirits, ghosts, angels and, later, in a presence much larger than all of those, a presence I can't reach with my five senses, though it usually reaches me. Although I haven't met anyone since I was four, I've heard voices on a number of occasions guiding and comforting me. I even survived one incident because Honya heard and obeyed.

After our summer romance at the Icefields, Honya returned to Simon Fraser University in Vancouver for a while. I went back to Edmonton, working part-time at Tana Brake and attending Alberta College to raise my high school average so I could attend university, too. I travelled to Vancouver every month in order to be with her, and it was during one of these visits that we decided to go to Stanley Park. It was October, 1967, and after taking the trolley bus all the way from Burnaby, around six o'clock and almost dark, we finally arrived at the now defunct bear cages.

"We gotta go," she said.

"What do you mean we gotta go? We just got here."

"If you don't come right now, I'm leaving without you." She turned, walking briskly away from the bear cages and heading out of the park.

I thought *what is it with this woman? I came all the way from Edmonton and now we're leaving!*

I didn't stand there long and soon caught up to her. "Why are we leaving?"

"Something told me we have to leave right now," she said. As I listened to the determination in her voice and her hurried footsteps, I asked: "What do you mean something told you?"

"Look, I'm not going to stop and explain things to you. We've gotta get outta here fast."

I was still no further ahead. *Something told her? I didn't see anything, I didn't hear anything. As a matter of fact, I was enjoying myself and find this a bit annoying. We've gotta get outta here fast?* I thought about pursuing it further but could see her resolve, so I dropped it.

We caught the trolley bus on Georgia Street, transferred at Granville, crossed the Granville Street Bridge, and ended up at a really neat pizza joint on Broadway. I'd never seen anything like it in Edmonton: a guy in a window above street level, twirling a large flat wheel of pizza dough, throwing it above his head, catching it again before it stopped spinning, then gracefully allowing the rotations come to a stop on the doughy counter. This was too cool! I love this girl!

After pizza, we made our way back to her apartment which was located below Simon Fraser on Hastings Street in Burnaby.

"Let's turn on the radio," I said.

An announcer came on with a flash newsbreak, interrupting The Beatles' *All You Need Is Love*: "We've just learned about a murder in Stanley Park. A man was brutally stabbed to death near the bear cages about six o'clock this evening."

Honya's mouth was slightly open as her clear blue eyes stared at me in disbelief. I felt coolness in the room as I started to perspire.

We couldn't talk right away, almost as if we had a moment of silence for the guy, and then we started speculating about who, why, would they've killed us if we saw something, and on and on. It didn't take us long before we realized we were very thankful to be alive; and I was utterly amazed how Honya was warned about this imminent danger and our possible death.

My first remembrance of a voice warning me of danger was after Honya and I separated. I was alone driving my 1980 Volkswagen Jetta across the High Level Bridge in Edmonton on my way to a weekly practice with the Richard Eaton Singers (this was the mid-1980s and I was singing tenor in a large, 160 voice, classical choir. We performed four concerts per year with the Edmonton Symphony, including *Handel's Messiah* at Christmas). I had just pulled onto the bridge. There wasn't a car in sight. My heart quickened as I down-shifted to second, floored the little four-banger, and shifted into third, listening to engine whine higher and louder as the rpm's approach the red line. I glanced at the speedometer and saw the needle pointing at 100 kilometres per hour.

I heard a gentle but firm voice say "slow down." I thought, *did I just hear something*, as I shifted into fourth and watched the needle approach 110. The voice lost all patience and shouted throughout my being: "SLOW DOWN!"

I hit the brakes hard, down-shifted to third, and caught a quick glimpse of the speedometer at 45 kilometres per hour when the car began to fish tail – it was above freezing all day, but I guess the conditions were just right that evening for black ice. The car almost spun out of control, but I pumped the brakes in staccato fashion, slid through both lanes at the end of the bridge, and somehow manoeuvred around the corner, just missing the curb and steel guard rail by millimetres. Although I tied to ignore that voice, I couldn't.

Julian Jayne's book, *The Origin of Consciousness in the Breakdown of the Bicameral Mind*, explains these kinds of voices basically as follows: man was unsubjective before the Iliad.

The ancients had an unsubjective, or fact oriented state more akin to a God oriented state, wherein God provided direction for action and decision. The evolution of consciousness has brought more values into contemporary thought. Given my experiences, it seems we may have retained some of this ability, albeit reduced, to listen like the ancients.

During the 1980s, I was going through the Christian phase of my Spiritual journey. I adopted the teachings as I knew, since I was four, there was a Spirit world. The Christians seemed to have an explanation for it. Although I went to church, sang in the choir (I even graduated to singing with Richard Eaton), prayed in tongues, and listened to the sermons, there were two teachings I felt very uncomfortable with. One was the teaching that the only way to God is through Jesus Christ; and, over time, the second one was the teaching that all homosexual behaviour is sin and an abomination to God. I had always felt there were a number of ways (some of them religious) to reach God, as well as a number of ways (often not religious) that He reached you. These feelings were substantiated when I read Tom Harpur's *The Pagan Christ,* wherein he, a learned Christian theologian teaching for years at the college level, exposed many of the Christian teachings as bogus, not just through opinion and Bible "interpretation" (as seems to be the practice in Christian circles), but through extensive new research and empirical evidence going back 4,000 years to Egypt. Although it may not seem likely, I actually found this book to increase my belief in a Presence, a Creator, a Universe, an Energy that is much larger than me (I don't like using the word "God" because people's preconceived ideas about its meaning). I'm not anti-Christian or against their teachings, I just can't accept all their teachings. Writers like Tom Harpur and others with more knowledge and wisdom than myself feel the same.

My feelings about homosexuality were initially in line with the Christians I was brought up with. I even knew specific passages from the book of Romans in the Bible and drew on quotes about homosexuality being an abomination to God. However, I also learned a lot about letting God be the judge in all situations, with quotes like "judge not, lest ye be judged," (Luke 6:37), and learned that God pours out unconditional love.

In the mid '90s I was living in Vernon, B.C. and started jamming in a little club downtown on weekends and some weekday nights. I really enjoyed playing guitar, singing, playing drums, and some nights even got to play bass. The owner of the club was a gay woman, Dora, who not only welcomed me, but went out of her way to give me hugs whenever I came to jam. I got to know Dora after a while and, although she could be a very hard lady to work with (as some of her employees and minor partners told me), I talked to her quite a lot and watched as she expressed a universal love for people and animals (she raised horses and one night told me how beautiful it was she was able to help with the birth of a colt). I had never experienced or observed such universal love before – it was truly unconditional. She expressed this unconditional love for me too, knowing full well I was a straight guy. I thought *if Dora can express love unconditionally to people and animals so freely, why can't I? Who am I to judge her or anyone else who is a lesbian or a homosexual?* Since I met Dora, I no longer sit as judge and jury about homosexuality and have recently learned that many First Nation teachings celebrate the "two-spirited," or "double-spirited" person as a special individual with insight and knowledge, often teaching others how to act harmoniously with both sexes.

Presently, I don't align myself with any particular faith and feel content to be a soul full of life energy contained in a body, connected to the universe. Looking at my aging physical self, I can't help thinking of a high school physics class, where I learned the law: "energy cannot be created nor destroyed." When my physical self dies, I believe my life energy returns to the universe. My present energy connection with other human beings, plants, animals, even the mountains, as well as the broader universe, feels akin to the teachings of my First Nation ancestors. These teachings allow me to express my beliefs freely, beyond the restrictions of a doctrinal box. I've felt free enough to spend a five-day retreat of silence and meditation with the Buddhists, visit a Hindu temple and receive a prayer bracelet, attend a Hare Krishna service and sharing a meal with them. Recently, I even attended, a four-day fast (no food or water, just a quart of herbal tea every twenty-four hours) followed by a sweat, an annual fast over four-years, which is a First Nation Vision Quest.

To this day, voices continue to speak to me whether I'm on a conscious Spiritual quest or not. During my first four-day Vision Quest fast, my Medicine Woman, Trudy Jack, listened while I told her about my vision as we sat in the Sweat Lodge: "women's voices outside my tent coming to visit me." She interpreted these voices (there were two or three of them) as those of my grandmother and great grandmothers, happily saying something like: "well, look who is back with us today." During the first year of the new millennium, I was walking alone along English Bay in Vancouver when another voice came to me and said "write your memoir." Although I tried to ignore this voice, it kept coming back stronger until, well— you've just read what an insistent voice can do. I believe we all hear them. We just have to listen and obey.

EPILOGUE

IT'S MARCH 2014 AND I'M ENJOYING A balmy, briny breeze off the South Atlantic in Uruguay. I've fallen in love with a beautiful, passionate Uruguayan lady and sitting on the second floor balcony of her home located on the coast, about 240 kilometres east of Montevideo. Elena and I attempt to live years of continuous summer – travelling back and forth between Canada and Uruguay. I'm currently going through a second divorce which should come to a close later this year. After this second time around (with infidelity of my second wife), I thought I would never fall in love again. There's no telling the future and I am happy and thankful to be in love and to be loved again.

I inherited mom and dad's home in Kelowna, British Columbia in 2013. Looking after mom during the last eight months of her life was a privilege; she died of bowl cancer at age 89, June 27, 2013. Mom (Christina Bernadette Shennan, nee Callihoo) did not suffer a lot and I'm thankful to have spent the time with her cooking meals (although I'm not much of a cook) and talking of our lives. Mom was lucid right to the end and only stopped driving a couple of months before she died. "I feel like I have a fever, but know I don't have one, so I'm not going to drive anymore and the car is yours!" she said.

We had a wonderful celebration of life for mom with the BC Old Time Fiddlers playing many favourite tunes and some people even danced – mom played guitar and piano accompaniment with the fiddlers for 25 years. About eighty friends and relatives came to mom's celebration, including her first cousin and best friend Tina who recently turned 90. Tina was brought to the celebration by her daughter Margaret Ann (who now looks after my new home when I'm in Uruguay). The day after the celebration, Aunt Betty and I spread mom's ashes beside dad's ashes on a golf course north of Kelowna. Although it's illegal to spread ashes on a golf course, "we never had this conversation," said the course manager.

Dad, William Shennan, died of heart failure at age 82 in March, 2004. He had Graves' disease (hyperactive thyroid) when he was 70, undiagnosed for two years, which I believe damaged his heart. I'm very thankful mom and dad's ashes are now together.

I've recently completed a nine year stint at Indian and Northern Affairs Canada in Vancouver (re-named Aboriginal Affairs and Northern Development Canada) and became "job free" in September, 2012. I'm not "retired" (I don't like the word; it sounds like a life of not knowing what to do without a job). My time at Indian Affairs was fulfilling, having spent many days working with First Nations on the Rez doing Comprehensive Community Planning. It felt like I was repeating parts of my earlier life as a child growing up in two places – spending half of my time on the Rez and half in the city.

The job was refreshing because we did not administer a "program" designed by mandarins in Ottawa who thought they knew what was best for First Nations. Instead, we went to First Nations, asked them if they were interested in Comprehensive Community Planning, and when they said yes, assembled funds from various programs, including the Regional Director General's slush fund. Over a four year period a group of four, and at times five of us, were able to direct over $12 million dollars to First Nations in British Columbia! It was very fulfilling. The plans, if done well, helped First Nations take control of their destiny and gradually break away from the confines of the colonial **Indian Act**. It was one of the highlights of my career as a Community Planner.

Before my time at Indian Affairs, I've had one business and various jobs, including the Executive Director of the South Peace Regional Planning Commission in Grande Prairie, Alberta. The job lasted only three years since all 10 Planning Commissions in Alberta were closed in 1995, ending a 40 year history of sound land use planning encompassing the whole province. For me, it was a good three years and I'm thankful I had to move on and not end my career by "retiring" from that job as I had originally planned.

I'm still singing and playing guitar, writing a few songs, and enjoy performing occasional gigs at coffee houses. In the last few years I've teamed up with my old buddy John McCallum. John asked me to join him busking on the seawall in Victoria and I've also learned some of his new tunes (he has some excellent and professional CDs and has spent time in Nashville). Gord Forster bought a new guitar after not playing for 30 years, so now John, Gord, and I get together to gig, much like it was at the "ice" and in Giuseppe's pizza joint in Edmonton almost 50 years ago! Before this recent reunion, I had lost touch completely with John and Gord. It's good to be playing music with them again. All three of us have moved to British Columbia, so it's easier to get together once in a while. As for skiing, I did it for 32 winters in a row, but no more. Running, riding a bike, and going to the gym three times a week have replaced the slopes. My dad was a real golfer and I golfed with him when he was alive, but have since sold my clubs. Never did break that magic 100, meanwhile dad was always a consistent low 80's golfer.

Brian MacKenzie owns a sign business (Fast Signs) in Minneapolis – St. Paul, Minnesota. He, like me, has been through two marriages and recently married a third time to a lovely lady, Bernadette. *He sure has faith in that institution,* I used to think, but that was before I met Elena. Brian was in Jasper in 2011 with Bernadette, and at a small gathering of friends around a campfire, I was thrilled to sing and play guitar again – as it was in the old Jasper when we worked at the 'ice' almost 50 years ago. Gord

Forster and his wife Karen were there too, along with Gerry Shea and his wife Bev. I think that's when Gord decided to play guitar again. As for Brian, I think he intends to pick up the guitar after a long hiatus. He no longer skis (like me), but golf has replaced his passion. He gets together with Gerry Shea for golf sessions and they sometimes volunteer at PGA tournaments. I'm very thankful Brian's cancer has been remission for nine years now. He is able to enjoy his life so fully.

Gerry Shea lives north of Kelowna on Shuswap Lake. Lately, we see each other about once per year. He works as a geologist, mostly in the oil and gas fields of Alberta, and says his "job free" days are imminent. Every time I try to get together with him he's off on another 18 hour a day assignment on a frozen field near Rimbey, Alberta. The last time we got together, Grant Cameron joined us. He also lives near me in Vernon, BC (seems like all Albertans eventually end up in BC). Grant has a recycling business, amongst other interests in Alberta, and spends a lot of time travelling between provinces. He still loves skiing and lives beside the road to Silver Star Ski Resort. Grant also loves golf. He and Gerry enjoy the links around Vernon.

When we were in Jasper in 2011, we met up with Terry Harris. He has had many successful businesses in Jasper, including a gas station and a ski shop. Jasper has been his home for nearly 50 years and he still skis every winter. He told me he doesn't like golfing. Terry also said Gordon Harper has been living in Victoria since the '70s and volunteering with a group of people assisting those with addictions. Gordon has come through some difficult times and is now helping others. He has been recognized publicly for his tireless efforts.

Aunt Helen, now 87, lives alone in her home in the Holyrood neighbourhood of Edmonton, but enjoys frequent visits by her son Sandy, her grandchildren and great grandchildren. Uncle Ted Pywell has Alzheimer's and is sadly in a home deteriorating. Elena and I visited Helen in 2013 and we enjoyed our visit talking of old times and looking at old pictures. Helen is the family historian for the Shennan family. It was a joy to share some of my memoir with her. Aunt Bessie, my dad's second sister, died of Alzheimer's in 2012 after being in a home for almost 10 years. Uncle Bill Jenkins, her husband and my uncle, who drove the grader when I was a kid in Rossdale, died of cancer in 1986. Uncle Robert Shennan, who rescued me from a dance at the Noyes Hall in Calahoo when I was 11, died near his 65th birthday in 1999. He was renovating his country home shortly after he became "job free" when mice ran out of the walls. I believe he died of Hantavirus.

Gramma, Lottie Callihoo (nee Fyfe), died at age 93 in Vernon, BC, 1996. She had dementia in her final years and trouble recognizing me and others. Other than arthritis, she did not seem to have other serious illnesses. Grampa, Solomon Timothy Callihoo, died of natural causes in Vernon, BC, 1986, and was just a few weeks short of reaching his 88th birthday. Mom, Gramma, and I were with him the moment he died. About two weeks before, he said to me "I've had enough, it's time to go."

Mom said something similar before she died in 2013. Granddad, Alexander Henderson Shennan, died of bowl cancer in Edmonton, Alberta, 1956 when I was nine years old. I faintly remember his thick Scottish brogue.

For others, my information is limited to what I can obtain on the internet and through my casual discussions with friends and relatives. Aunt Betty and her partner Jim Kam are exceptions, of course, since they are my neighbours in Kelowna. We get together about once a week when Elena and I are in Canada. We have a meal or just visit and watch sports on TV. Betty has arthritis problems, like Gramma did, and now has one artificial hip (thankfully I did not inherit the arthritis genes; Grampa and mom did not have aches or pains either). Betty's four children are equally split between Alberta and BC and she enjoys her seven grandchildren. Uncle Les Gerlat, Betty's first husband, father of her children and my farming mentor when I was 12, died in 1980 before he reached his 50th birthday. As for my son, Waylon, he lives a peaceful and fulfilled life in Alberta.

Wayne Callihoo, my cousin, lives with his wife Helen in Airdrie Alberta. They have four children, I believe, so he must at least be a grandfather now. I last talked to Wayne at a wedding in 1986.

Russ L'Hirondelle, my cousin, lives in Grande Prairie, Alberta with his wife Randa. Russ and I spent time together when I lived in Grande Prairie in the early '90s, but we have since lost touch again. Russ is a grandfather and maybe a great grandfather by now, since Russ and Randa had five children. Russ's brother Charlie lives in Winterburn, Alberta and I sometimes see him when I attend the Michel Band meetings (we aren't officially recognized by Aboriginal Affairs, but you can't eliminate our Treaty Rights!).

Susan Jamieson Petley-Jones, my grade six crush, has become my friend on Facebook in 2014. She's married, a grandmother, lives in Surrey, BC and has a summer cottage on Shuswap Lake near Gerry Shea. It's nice to be in touch again.

Peter Uram I have not talked since high school, but Grant Cameron sees him and manages some of Pete's property in Edmonton. Pete lives in Vancouver and initiated one of Vancouver's first community pubs.

Occasionally, I would visit with Sid Sugarman when I lived in Edmonton in the 1980s. He took time off being a teacher and was managing a restaurant. Sid was another one of those guys who kept growing after high school and didn't stop until six foot one or two. I haven't talked to Sid since then.

Philip Lovell, my childhood buddy from "The Block," died of cancer at age 63. The last time I remember seeing him was just after high school, but recently Elena and I got together with his two sisters, Donna and Myrna, and it was nice to share some old memories. We met in the apartment of Lucie Evans in the old apartment block where I grew up, and her son Tom and daughter Debbie joined us, too. Although arthritis makes moving difficult, Lucie was as vibrant and talkative as ever at her 90 plus years. She still writes poetry and even shared some with us. Lucie told us Patrick Vandergaag, another childhood friend, died when he was 61.

Inge Stauning, my pretty "sister" from the '60s, is a realtor in Ontario, according to the internet. I haven't talked to her since the '60s. As for the other girls she used to hang around with, like Joan Ullman, Heather Cochran, and Linda Hadley, they probably have married names since I haven't located them.

Terry Chapman, another childhood buddy from "The Block," recently became "job free," according to the internet. He worked for the City of Edmonton for years, but I haven't talked to Terry since the '70s when he owned a house beside me in the Highlands neighbourhood of Edmonton.

Gilbert Todd, my old Métis buddy from the Flats, died in 2013. I contacted Gilbert through Facebook in 2010 and he and his daughter Jacquie assisted me in researching Bobby Todd's fatal car accident. I was fortunate enough to visit Gilbert in 2011 and, although not healthy, we spent hours talking of old times. We had not seen each other since high school.

Bob Clarke, my old guitar teacher, died in the late '90s. Bob was the lead guitar player for Wes Dakus and the Rebels in the early '60s. Wes Dakus died of cancer at 75 in 2012.

I may have missed some and for that I apologize. I hope you still enjoyed the memoir. As for my other audience, meaning relatives not yet born, I hope you enjoy this memoir, too. I often think how exciting it would be to read a first-hand account from an ancient grandfather who paddled 4,000 kilometres in a birch bark canoe across Canada in the 1790s; or a distant uncle who escaped from France wearing a white shirt as a Huguenot in the 1500s. My life has not been as exciting as some of my past relatives' lives, but this is a first-hand account of a life from 1949 to 1968, with a few extra experiences bringing us up to 2014. I hope you learn something reading my memoir, my future relatives. It's a part of you. Enjoy!

REFERENCES

Books / Discussions / Magazines / Papers / Web-sites:

1. Alberta Online Encyclopaedia (2010) www.abheritage.ca
    Elders' Voices – Pehonan (Rossdale Flats)

2. Alberta Railway Museum, (2009) www.railwaymuseum.ab.ca
    24215 – 34 street, Edmonton, AB, Canada

3. Alec, Elaine (2009) Discussion regarding the "Child Centred
    Society," Penticton Indian Band, Penticton, BC

4. Barnard, John (2006) Excerpt from the 2006 Documentary
    featuring an interview with Ethnomusicologist Lynn Whidden;
    see YouTube – *Sierra's Song-Métis Fiddle Music*

5. BC Archives (2010) www.bcarchives.gov.bc.ca A Brief History
    of the Doukhobors in BC

6. Bopp, Michael and Judy Bopp (2006), *Recreating the World,
    A Practical Guide to Building Sustainable Communities*,
    second edition, Four Worlds Press, Calgary, Alberta

7. Calihoo, Robert and Robert Hunter (1991) *Occupied
    Canada, A Young White Man Discovers His Unsuspected
    Past*, McClelland & Stewart Inc. Toronto

8. Cardinal, Harold (1969) *The Unjust Society*, Douglas & McIntyre, Vancouver, BC Canada

9. Deakin, Jack (1960) *Four Killed In Car Wreck*, The Edmonton Journal Newspaper (microfiche) Edmonton, Alberta

10. EPCOR's History (2009) www.epcor.ca

11. Evans, Lucie, (circa 2000) *The Soul of a Building*, in *Verses*, International Poet Society

12. Gandhi, Mahatma (1927) *The Story of My Experiments with Truth, An Autobiography*, General Press, New Delhi (2009 edition)

13. Granger, Marcel (2010) *Bombardier B-12 CS Multi-Passenger Snowmobile*, www.lino.com

14. Hatcher, Colin K. and Tom Schwarzkopf, (1983) *Edmonton's Electric Transit: The Storey of Edmonton's Streetcars and Trolley Buses*, Railfare Enterprises Limited, Ontario

15. Harpur, Tom, (2004) *The Pagan Christ, Recovering The Lost Light*, Thomas Allen Publishers, Toronto

16. Herzog, Lawrence (2002) The *School Named for Donald Ross*, The Realtors Association of Edmonton, Edmonton, Alberta

17. Herzog, Lawrence (2004) *At the Birthplace of Edmonton*, The Realtors Association of Edmonton, Edmonton, Alberta

18. Herzog, Lawrence (2006) *The Ross Flats Apartments*, The Realtors Association of Edmonton, Edmonton, Alberta

19. Hefner, Hugh, (1953) *Playboy*, an American Men's Magazine founded in Chicago, Illinois in 1953, now part of Playboy Enterprises Inc.

Wesley Shennan

20. Imai, Shin and Jessica Feldman, (2007) *Indian Act and Aboriginal Constitutional Provisions*, Statutes of Canada Annotated, Thompson Carswel

21. Jaynes, Julian (1976) *The Origin of Consciousness in the Breakdown of the Bicameral Mind*, Penguin Books

22. Kashyap, Rina (2005) *The Subversion of the Colonial System of Humiliation: A Case Study of the Gandhian Strategy*, Chairperson, Department of Journalism, LSR, Delhi University/Fulbright Scholar, Centre for Justice and Peace building, Eastern Mennonite University, Virginia. For a further exposition of colonialism as a living civilizing mission see Nandy, Ashis The Intimate Enemy: Loss and Recovery of Self under Colonialism Delhi,OUP 1983; Said, Edward Orientalism New York: Pantheon, 1978; Sardar, Ziauddin Orientalism Philadelphia, PA: Open University Press, 1999; Fisher-Tine, Harald and Michael Mann Colonialism as Civilizing Mission: Cultural Ideology in British India London: Anthem Press, 2004.

23. Lederman, Ann (2010) *Fiddling*, The Canadian Encyclopaedia / the Encyclopaedia of Music in Canada, www.thecanadianencylopedia.com

24. Lederman, Ann (1987) *Old Native and Métis Fiddling in Manitoba*, Vol. 1, Falcon Productions, 83 A. Queen Street West, Toronto, Ontario M6J 1G1

25. MacPherson, Elizabeth, (1998) *The Sun Traveller, The Story of the Callihoos In Alberta*, Musee Heritage Museum, 5 St. Anne Street St. Albert, Alberta

26. McEachern, Terrance (2010) *Aboriginal student pride important, say residential school survivors*, Northern News Services, Published Wednesday, October 13, 2010

27. Miller, J.R. (1996) *Shingwauk's Vision: A History of Native Residential Schools*, University of Toronto Press, Toronto, Ontario

28. Musee Heritage Museum (2009) *Cascading Pedigree*, Callihoo Family research, Musee Heritage Museum, 5 St. Anne Street, St. Albert, Alberta

29. Moore, Thomas (1998) The Soul of Sex, HarperCollins Publishers Inc., New York

30. Petersen, Robert E (1948) Hot Rod, a magazine originally published by Petersen Publishing Company, published by Robert Burkle's Source Interlink since 2007

31. Pywell, Helen (1979) A.H. Shennan Family, Michael School District #4404, an article written for a school district publication

32. Solicitor General Canada and the Aboriginal Healing Foundation, (2002) The final report of a First Nation Research Project on Healing in Canadian Aboriginal Communities, Mapping The Healing Journey, APC 21 CA (2002)

33. Struzik, Ed (2005) The Dunbow School: A blueprint for despair, The Shingwauk Project, Shingwauk News, estruzik@thejournal.canwest.com

34. The Canadian Encyclopedia (2010) Native People, Education, www.thecanadianencyclopedia.com

35. Vernon, Jamie, (2006) Great White Noise Magazine Presents The Canadian Pop Encyclopaedia, http://jam.canoe.ca/music/pop.encyclopedia/D/Dakus_Wes.html

36. www.wikipedia.org History of the Poma Lift

37. Wood, Daniel (2010) Discussion and assistance in re-organization and ideas for re-writing memoir

Music:

1. Berry, Chuck (1956) *Roll Over Beethoven*, Chess Records

2. Blackwell, Robert "Bumps," Enotris Johnson, Richard Penniman ("Little Richard"), (1956) *Long Tall Sally*, Specialty Records; Recorded by the Beatles (1964), Parlophone Records (UK); Capitol Records, Canada, Catalogue T6063

3. Bogle, Bob (1960) *Walk Don't Run*, The Ventures, Blue Horizon Label

4. Cash, Johnny, (1958) *I Still Miss Someone*, Columbia, John Carter Cash Publisher

5. Cash, Johnny and Gordon Jenkins (1955) *Folsom Prison Blues*, produced by Sam Phillips, Sun Records

6. Clarke, Bob (1964) *Las Vegas Scene*, Wes Dakus and the Rebels, Quality Records 6120LP, also YouTube, posted July 17, 2009 CFRN 2/3 TV Marquee: Barry Allen & The Rebels, Part Three; *Las Vegas Scene*, featuring Bob Clarke on Guitar; *Rain Drops*, sung by Barry Allen; and comments by band members in 1993.

7. Cooke, Sam (1957) *Your Send Me*, Keen Records, an imprint of RCA Victor

8. Dylan, Bob (1964) *One Too Many Mornings*, Columbia Album: The Times They Are a-Changin'

9.   Fireballs, The (1959, 1960, 1961) *Torquay, Vaquero, Gunshot*, Top Rank Record Company, re-issued on Ace Records (UK), and Sundazed Records (US)

10. Garland, Joe and Andy Razaf, (1929) *In The Mood*, Glenn Miller's Big Band recording RCA Victor, 1939

11. Guthrie, Woody (1930) *It Takes a Worried Man To Sing a Worried Song*, Woody Guthrie Publications

12. Handel, George Frederic (1741) *Messiah*, now referred to as *Handel's Messiah*, an Oratorio recorded by numerous choirs and orchestras

13. Horton, Johnny and Tillman Franks (1958) *When It's Spring Time In Alaska (It's Forty Below)*, Columbia

14. Jagger, Mick and Keith Richards,(1965) *(I Can't Get No) Satisfaction*, The Rolling Stones, Decca Records, London 45-LIN9766(US)

15. Karas, Anton (1949) *The Third Man Theme*, Decca Recording, Catalogue Number 24839

16. Lennon, John and Paul McCartney (1967) *All You Need Is Love*, The Beatles, Parlophone Records, UK

17. Lightfoot, Gordon (1966) *Early Morning Rain, For Lovin' Me, Long River*, United Artists Album: Lightfoot! Catalogue Number UAS - 6487

18. Merrill, Bob (1952) *How Much Is That Doggy in the Window*, recorded by Patti Page, 1952, Mercury Records, Catalogue Number 70070

19. Richards, Cliff, Jerry Lordan and the Shadows (1960) *Dance On*, EMI Records

20. Traditional Métis Fiddle Tune (circa 1830) *The Red River Jig*

21. Traditional Fiddle Tune (circa 1900) *The Old Man and the Old Woman*

22. Wiseman, Scotty, (1945) *Have I Told You Lately that I Love You?* RCA Victor Catalogue No: CDN-5122

Movies:

1. *Backbeat* (1994), PolyGram Filmed Entertainment, directed by Iain Softley, dramatization of the Hamburg, Germany phase of the Beatles' early history.

2. *Little Big Man* (1970), The American Film Institute, directed by Arthur Penn, contrasts the lives of American Pioneers and Native Americans, contains a clear social conscience about prejudice and injustice.

Photographs:

1. Engler, Bruno (1967) Ski Pictorial, featuring ski area at Lake Louise, Alpine Films, Box 832 Banff, Alberta

2. Van Loon, Jake (1954) Grades three and four, Donald Ross Elementary School, Edmonton, Alberta

CPSIA information can be obtained
at www.ICGtesting.com
Printed in the USA
LVHW020340180719
624447LV00001B/31